AF885045

# Advancing Transparency in the U.S. Department of Homeland Security

## Defining the Office of Homeland Security Statistics

JOHN BORDEAUX, JOSHUA SIMULCIK, LAURA BELLOWS, RAYMOND KUO, JOHN S. HOLLYWOOD, MICHELLE D. ZIEGLER, RYAN CONSAUL, DAVID STEBBINS, ERIN N. LEIDY, KARISHMA R. MEHTA, JO CAULKINS, NANCY HUERTA

HSOAC
HOMELAND SECURITY
OPERATIONAL ANALYSIS CENTER

This research was published in 2024.

# About This Report

The Secretary of Homeland Security issued an action memorandum on July 25, 2022, instructing the Under Secretary of the Office of Strategy, Policy, and Plans to "establish an independent Office of Homeland Security Statistics (OHSS) as a recognized statistical unit within the Department of Homeland Security."[1] Delegation 23037 authorized OHSS's purpose and role as being "to perform homeland security statistical activities and independent statistical reporting for the Department."[2]

OHSS was established in September 2023 as the department's statistical office in accordance with the Foundations for Evidence-Based Policymaking Act of 2018 but also with a mandate to qualify as a recognized statistical agency or unit under the Office of Information and Regulatory Affairs within the Office of Management and Budget (OMB). Before OHSS was created, the primary statistical activity, which was limited to the immigration information domain and not an OMB-recognized statistical agency, was the Office of Immigration Statistics in the Office of Strategy, Policy, and Plans. The inaugural executive director and existing staff transitioned to stand up OHSS.

This research was requested to address the challenges of establishing an independent statistical office to aid in decisionmaking and policy for DHS while operating independently of the department to provide authoritative data for public consumption. The findings should be of interest to stakeholders and customers of the federal statistical system.

This research was sponsored by OHSS and conducted in the Infrastructure, Immigration, and Security Operations Program of the RAND Homeland Security Research Division, which operates the Homeland Security Operational Analysis Center (HSOAC).

## About the Homeland Security Operational Analysis Center

The Homeland Security Act of 2002 authorizes the Secretary of Homeland Security, acting through the Under Secretary for Science and Technology, to establish one or more federally funded research and development centers (FFRDCs) to provide independent analysis of homeland security issues.[3] RAND operates HSOAC as an FFRDC for DHS under contract 70RSAT22D00000001.

The HSOAC FFRDC provides the government with independent and objective analyses and advice in core areas important to the department in support of policy development, decisionmaking, alternative approaches, and new ideas on issues of significance. HSOAC also works with and supports other federal, state, local, tribal, and public- and private-sector organizations that make up the homeland security enterprise. HSOAC's research is undertaken by mutual consent with DHS and organized as a set of discrete tasks. This report presents the results of research and analysis conducted under task order 70RDAD22FR0000119, Analytic Support to the Office of Immigration Statistics. The results presented in this report do not necessarily reflect official DHS opinion or policy.

---

[1] Robert Silvers, Under Secretary, Office of Strategy, Policy, and Plans; U.S. Department of Homeland Security (DHS), "Establishing an Office of Homeland Security Statistics," memorandum for the Secretary, July 25, 2022, p. 1.

[2] Robert Silvers, Under Secretary, Office of Strategy, Policy, and Plans; DHS, *Delegation to the Executive Director of the Office of Homeland Security Statistics*, Delegation 23037, revision 00, September 29, 2023, p. 1.

[3] Public Law 107-296, Homeland Security Act of 2002, November 25, 2002, § 305, Federally Funded Research and Development Centers; U.S. Code, Title 6, Domestic Security; Chapter 1, Homeland Security Organization; Subchapter III, Science and Technology in Support of Homeland Security; Section 185, Federally Funded Research and Development Centers.

For more information on the RAND Homeland Security Research Division, see www.rand.org/hsrd. For more information on this publication, see www.rand.org/t/RRA2444-1.

## Acknowledgments

We thank our sponsor, Marc Rosenblum, for his vision and support in facilitating interviews and his engagement throughout the course of this work, including hosting a workshop to collaboratively develop a logic model to guide OHSS strategy and operations. Within OHSS staff, we deeply appreciate the assistance of Thomas Woermer in helping us coordinate across OHSS leadership.

Within HSOAC, we thank Douglas C. Ligor, Joseph C. Chang, and Elina Treyger for their diligence and patience as the principal investigators for the overall study, of which this research represented one of several tasks. In addition, we benefited from thoughtful quality assurance reviews from RAND colleagues Paul Brenner and Jeremy M. Eckhause, and special thanks are due our esteemed external reviewer, Nancy Potok, former chief statistician of the United States.

Any errors in this report are our responsibility.

# Summary

In God we trust; all others must bring data.
—attributed to W. Edwards Deming

## Issue

A generation has passed since a federal statistical agency (FSA) was established in the United States in 1991, and several have existed for more than a century.[1] There are therefore few people alive with firsthand knowledge of successful approaches for establishing an FSA. In addition, the playing field has shifted considerably since 1991 in terms of statutory authority, executive guidance, technology tools for modeling and analysis, and internet technologies for dissemination and visualization, to name just a few changes. There is no playbook for standing up an FSA[2]—nor should this report be represented as providing such a playbook. Each FSA adapts to the needs of its parent agency and must build on the statutory language in the Foundations for Evidence-Based Policymaking Act of 2018 (commonly called the *Evidence Act*); executive guidance from OMB; and public works, such as *Principles and Practices for a Federal Statistical Agency*, to shape an activity that both serves the federal agency's need for information for improved decisionmaking and represents the public's interest in providing transparency into the parent agency.[3]

Although this report represents OHSS as starting from scratch, technically, the office's leadership, staff, and resources are drawn from the erstwhile Office of Immigration Statistics. That office operated in a single information domain and focused on providing authoritative data to assist departmental decisionmakers about immigration policy implementation. The OHSS expansion into multiple information domains,[4] representing operational and administrative data from across all DHS components, and adding the role of an independent RSAU under OMB likely mean that resources from the erstwhile Office of Immigration Statistics functions will represent a small fraction of future OHSS workload.

For OHSS, the task is to build on existing foundational elements and craft an office that represents a department with multiple mission areas and therefore multiple information domains. Other unique challenges for OHSS include the use of administrative and operational data as inputs to statistical analysis and no direct collection of data on the part of OHSS: Its role is to provide analysis, modeling, and reporting of component statistical data.

[1] Throughout this report, we use *FSA*, *principal statistical agency*, and *recognized statistical agency or unit* (*RSAU*) interchangeably to represent the Office of Homeland Security Statistics' (OHSS's) status as an Office of Management and Budget (OMB)-recognized statistical agency, as contrasted with *agency statistical official*, which indicates OHSS's internal role for the U.S. Department of Homeland Security (DHS).

[2] A proposed OMB "trust directive" we reviewed during this study (OMB, "Statistical Policy Directive No. 1: Fundamental Responsibilities of Federal Statistical Agencies and Recognized Statistical Units," *Federal Register*, Vol. 79, No. 231, December 2, 2014 [notice of final decision]) would be a great advance toward a definition and purpose of an FSA.

[3] Committee on National Statistics; Division of Behavioral and Social Sciences and Education; National Academies of Sciences, Engineering, and Medicine, *Principles and Practices for a Federal Statistical Agency*, 7th ed., National Academies Press, 2021.

[4] Additional information domains include law enforcement, international trade, cybersecurity, emergency management, infrastructure protection, maritime, and screening.

The Homeland Security Operational Analysis Center was tasked to assist the executive director of OHSS in operationalizing the delegation of authority. In turn, we worked to answer specific research questions, including these:

- What can be learned from existing analyses and open-source materials about the federal statistical system?
- How can OHSS provide value to the components, in terms of both burden-sharing and advancing component statistical capacity and capabilities?
- Who are the internal and external stakeholders that will engage with OHSS, and what are their goals, objectives, and likely challenges?
- What tasks are associated with establishing an organization, and how should OHSS approach each of these establishing tasks?
- What are the organizational inputs, outputs, outcomes, stakeholders, and activities that link OHSS activities to strategic objectives or mission goals?

## Approach

We conducted a substantial literature review and interviewed dozens of current and former statistical officials to develop input for a detailed logic model and an organizational design framework.[5] In fall 2023, we presented these draft models for validation at a workshop attended by OHSS staff and representatives from DHS component statistical activities. These insights informed a draft mission statement, supporting strategy pillars and objectives, a target operating model, and draft implementation guidance.

## Observations Influencing Mission and Strategy

In the early months of this study, we observed several issues with which the newly created office will likely grapple—these observations emerged from the literature, interviews with FSA principals, and presentations and on-site conversations during the Federal Committee on Statistical Methodology 2023 Research and Policy Conference:

- There is an inherent tension for an FSA in operating as the department statistical office while maintaining its independence from its parent agency, but there are also specific organizational behaviors and protocols that can provide that independence to maintain public trust.
- The federal statistical system is working to balance the need for transparent government data with the protection of individual privacy. Statistical data are inherently designed to be unidentifiable—or, if they are identifiable, they must be protected. Either option ensures that personal information is obscured from public view. Importantly, statistical data that are identifiable cannot be used for operational purposes (e.g., benefit consideration, law enforcement). Although the primary guidance comes from the Privacy Act and emphasizes the importance of privacy, it does not focus solely on avoiding the identification of individuals. Instead, it underscores that privacy is a central concern while leaving the broader definition of *statistical purpose* open to interpretation.

[5] Our logic model follows the principles of McKinsey's 7-S model: shared values (or superordinate goal), skills, style, staff, structure, strategy, and systems. For more on this model, see Tom Peters, "A Brief History of the 7-S ('McKinsey 7-S') Model," blog post, January 9, 2011.

- OHSS faces challenges that are unique, not encountered by existing RSAUs:
  - OHSS will not capture data directly but rather will develop statistical products informed by both administrative and operational data from among DHS components, crossing multiple domains aligned with the DHS mission set.
  - OHSS needs to coordinate with DHS component statistical offices; establish productive relationships; and, finally, develop guidance, standard operating procedures, and protocols to scaffold these relationships and therefore ensure continued success under future leadership.
  - OHSS will provide both decision support and public reporting.
  - OHSS is starting from scratch as the first new FSA in more than a generation.

## Recommendations: Crafting a Target Operating Model for the Office of Homeland Security Statistics

We derived our recommendations from a methodical approach of reviewing existing literature and practices, gathering input from subject-matter experts and stakeholders, developing draft frameworks, validating them through a DHS-hosted workshop, and then synthesizing the findings into specific recommendations for OHSS's mission, strategy, and implementation plan. The strategic framework does not inform the shape of the organizational chart but provides goals and metrics for the activities of the professional staff:

- Develop and promulgate the following mission statement: "Foster transparency and data-driven homeland security decision-making by analyzing and disseminating timely, objective DHS data and statistics."[6]
- Adopt the following strategic pillars and objectives detailed herein to communicate OHSS's approach to its mission and how to measure its success:
  - Maintain the official DHS statistical system of record.
  - Provide statistical data services to mature the department's statistical activities.
  - Produce independent reports as an RSAU.
- Follow up on implementation tasks and implied policy guidance aligned with the target operating model. Details of a recommended approach and proposals for consideration are included in Chapter 6, "Implementation Plan."
- Develop policy guidance to define authorities and responsibilities that components will regain.
- Develop policy guidance to address data standardization and analytic modeling and visualization for consistent data representation.
- Establish OHSS role and responsibilities by
  - mapping OHSS leadership positions and managerial roles to specific authorities and requirements
  - developing end-to-end mapping of OHSS's assets, information flows, and decision processes
  - establishing measurable lines of effort outlining OHSS's role in enabling component data analysis and reporting
  - drafting standard operating procedures for data requests to ensure compliance with legal reporting requirements.
- Partner with the chief data officer.
- Support evidence-based policymaking.

6 OHSS has already adopted this. We include it in this report to represent a recommendation that might apply to future FSA organizations and to provide a full record of our analysis.

- Advise on statistical policies and procedures by
  - developing policy for independent report clearance, review, and release
  - establishing a directive outlining the scope for component review of OHSS products
  - establishing a structure for communicating data governance approaches from DHS policy offices.
- Ensure statistical confidentiality by verifying that information is used exclusively for statistical purposes under a pledge of confidentiality and prepare required annual reports to OMB.

OHSS might seek to identify near-term priorities to address in its next budget request and mid- and long-term priorities to address in future budget requests. It might also develop performance measures to track the implementation of its priorities.

The sponsor organization has been proactive in adopting and implementing several of the recommendations outlined in this report. Many of the proposed recommendations were embraced and actualized during our work, while others are currently undergoing implementation processes. As a result, readers might observe that some of the recommendations discussed as future proposals have already been realized or are visibly in progress. This responsive approach exemplifies the sponsor's commitment to continuous improvement and its receptiveness to the insights derived from this collaborative effort.

## Establish the Office of Homeland Security Statistics' Role and Responsibilities

We propose initiatives under objective 1.1 of the strategy (see Chapter 3) to clearly define OHSS's authorities, responsibilities, and decisionmaking processes within DHS. These include the following:

- Map OHSS leadership positions and managerial roles to specific authorities and requirements (initiative 1.1.3).
- Develop end-to-end mapping of OHSS's assets, information flows, and decision processes (initiative 1.1.4).
- Establish measurable lines of effort outlining OHSS's role in enabling component data analysis and reporting (initiative 1.1.5).
- Draft standard operating procedures for data requests to ensure compliance with legal reporting requirements (initiative 1.1.6).

## Partner with the Chief Data Officer

For objective 1.2, we recommend developing guidance for OHSS to partner with the DHS chief data officer on managing data elements and mechanisms per 44 U.S.C. § 3520 requirements (initiative 1.2.1).

## Support Evidence-Based Policymaking

Objective 1.4 focuses on producing and disseminating timely statistical information to support evidence-based policymaking and leadership decisions, in accordance with the Foundations for Evidence-Based Policymaking Act of 2018 (initiative 1.4.1).

## Advise on Statistical Policies and Procedures

We propose initiatives under objective 2.1 for OHSS to advise on statistical policies, techniques, and procedures, including the following:

- Develop policy for independent report clearance, review, and release (initiative 2.1.1).
- Establish a directive outlining the scope for component review of OHSS products (initiative 2.1.2).
- Establish a structure for communicating data governance approaches from DHS policy offices (initiative 2.1.3).

## Ensure Statistical Confidentiality

Objective 3.1 emphasizes following procedures established in OMB Confidential Information Protection and Statistical Efficiency Act guidance, such as the following:

- Verify that information is used exclusively for statistical purposes under a pledge of confidentiality (initiative 3.1.2).
- Prepare annual Confidential Information Protection and Statistical Efficiency Act reports to OMB (initiative 3.1.3).

# Contents

APPENDIXES

# Figures and Tables

## Figures



## Tables

# CHAPTER 1

# Introduction

## Motivation for This Study

The U.S. Department of Homeland Security (DHS) is significantly increasing its statistical capacity beginning in fiscal year (FY) 2024, establishing both an internal, agency-level statistical office, as specified in the Foundations for Evidence-Based Policymaking Act of 2018,[1] and a recognized statistical agency (i.e., a federal statistical agency [FSA]) reporting to the Office of Management and Budget (OMB) to operate as an addition to the extant FSAs that are covered by the Confidential Information Protection and Statistical Efficiency Act (CIPSEA), which was updated when reauthorized as part of the Evidence Act.[2] OHSS was authorized on September 29, 2023, through Delegation 23037, *Delegation to the Executive Director of the Office of Homeland Security Statistics*.[3]

In brief, OHSS will be dual-hatted, with responsibilities (1) to advance the department's statistical capacity and (2) to develop and disseminate statistical products independently of the department's influence or oversight. There are significant challenges to this undertaking, not the least of which is that OHSS is the first FSA to be established in a generation[4]—several of the current FSAs date back to the mid-19th century.

The sponsor implemented many of our recommendations during our work or is in the process of implementing them. As a result, readers might observe that some of the recommendations discussed as being proposed for the future are already being actualized or are visibly underway, a fact that reflects the dynamic and responsive nature of this work.

[1] Public Law 115-435, Foundations for Evidence-Based Policymaking Act of 2018, January 14, 2019.

[2] Public Law 107-347, E-Government Act of 2002; Title V, Confidential Information Protection and Statistical Efficiency Act, December 17, 2002. The reauthorization in Title III of the Evidence Act, Confidential Information Protection and Statistical Efficiency Act of 2018, is referred to as *CIPSEA 2018*.

Throughout this report, we use *FSA*, *principal statistical agency* (*PSA*), and *recognized statistical agency or unit* (*RSAU*) interchangeably to represent the Office of Homeland Security Statistics' (OHSS's) status as an OMB-recognized statistical agency, as contrasted with *agency statistical official* (*SO*), which indicates OHSS's internal role for DHS.

[3] Robert Silvers, Under Secretary, Office of Strategy, Policy, and Plans; DHS, *Delegation to the Executive Director of the Office of Homeland Security Statistics*, Delegation 23037, revision 00, September 29, 2023.

[4] The most recently launched FSA is the Bureau of Transportation Statistics, established in 1991. The last one created was the Bureau of Justice Statistics, established in 1979.

## Research Methods

We were tasked to assist the executive director in operationalizing the delegation of authority. In turn, we worked to answer specific research questions, among them the following:

- What can be learned from existing analyses and open-source materials about the federal statistical system (FSS)?
- How can OHSS provide value to the components, in terms of both burden-sharing and advancing component statistical capacity and capabilities?
- Who are the internal and external stakeholders that will engage with OHSS, and what are their goals, objectives, and likely challenges?
- What tasks are associated with establishing an organization, and how should OHSS approach each of these establishing tasks?
- What are the organizational inputs, outputs, outcomes, stakeholders, and activities that link OHSS activities to strategic objectives?
- What are the organizational inputs, outputs, outcomes, stakeholders, and activities that link activities to mission goals?

We used a variety of methods to address these research questions and related issues:

- We conducted an extensive literature review[5] to understand what can be learned from existing analyses and other open-source materials about what is expected from an OMB-recognized primary FSA and what principles exist to guide the development and operations of an RSAU.
- To explore the value OHSS can provide to the components, we conducted structured interviews as per protocols approved by RAND's institutional review board to understand the challenges that components face and how the components value OHSS. We also interviewed several former and current principals associated with the FSS to understand challenges and opportunities in standing up OHSS.
- We reviewed organizational engagement literature and heuristics to document the stakeholders that will engage with OHSS, as well as their goals, objectives, and likely challenges.
- We developed a target operating model to frame the implementation plan, using a specific organizational framework to detail which tasks are associated with establishing an organization and to understand how OHSS should approach each of these establishing tasks.
- We also developed a logic model (LM), validated through an in-person DHS workshop, to understand what OHSS should do and why.

---

[5] We focused on OMB directives (which establish guidance for RSAUs) and relevant legislation (e.g., the Foundations for Evidence-Based Policymaking Act of 2018, which updates and specifies roles for federal statistical officials (SOs). In addition, we reviewed sources, including one from the National Academies that provides authoritative principles for statistical offices (Committee on National Statistics [CNSTAT]; Division of Behavioral and Social Sciences and Education; National Academies of Sciences, Engineering, and Medicine, *Principles and Practices for a Federal Statistical Agency*, 7th ed., National Academies Press, 2021, also known as the *Purple Book*, now in its eighth edition). Using search terms to capture national-level statistic-keeping, we also reviewed foreign-government and intergovernmental guidance (e.g., Eurostat) for the management of government statistical activities. To learn about DHS data components, we reviewed component websites and RAND, DHS Office of Inspector General, Congressional Research Service (CRS), and U.S. Government Accountability Office (GAO) reports. For existing FSAs, sources included their websites, the Federal Committee on Statistical Methodology (FCSM) website, *Statistical Programs of the United States Government* reports, and the Purple Book, as well as relevant RAND, CRS, and GAO reports.

## Limitations

Although we used generally accepted methods for organizational analysis and design, DHS is unique in that many of its components predate the department itself and maintain an informal level of semi-autonomy that can often frustrate enterprise-level analyses and solutions. The department also has a broad mission and collects a variety of statistical information, including data on immigration, trade, disasters, terrorism, and cybersecurity. In addition, applying existing organizational analysis methods—developed for the private sector—to a public-sector organization requires some modification to incentives, metrics, and other non-monetary organizational characteristics.

Finally, as described in this report, the OHSS challenge is likewise unique and, in some ways, unprecedented in the FSS. Recommendations herein might need to be adapted to address emerging and unforeseen complications, including pending OMB guidance and, possibly, future directives on privacy and data management. One example might be that the best organizational structure would accommodate not only dual roles of department SO and RSAU but also the multiple information domains that align with the multiple department missions. Given the differences between OHSS and similar offices, some of the findings and recommendations might not be as relevant to other FSAs as they are to OHSS. Similarly, there might be alternatives that would be better suited to OHSS that have not been tried in statistical agencies with a narrower focus.

## Organization of This Report

This report is structured to document the journey involved in standing up OHSS. The remaining chapters are organized as follows:

- Chapter 2, "Background," presents an overview of the FSS and a brief discussion of current statistical activities at DHS.
- Chapter 3, "The Office of Homeland Security Statistics Mission and Strategy," presents, for OHSS review and validation, the pillars and supporting objectives that operationalize the mission statement adopted by OHSS following the workshop we held with DHS in fall 2023. Insights from this workshop were elicited within the frame of an LM.
- Chapter 4, "Office of Homeland Security Statistics Logic Model," describes the proposed LM, including major LOEs, inputs, and outcomes. The LM also addresses stakeholders, and a stakeholder engagement section goes into more detail on how to identify and engage stakeholders.
- Chapter 5, "Stakeholder Engagement," describes OHSS stakeholder groups and constructs.
- Chapter 6, "Implementation Plan," presents a target operating model informed by a commonly used organizational lens or framework. A target operating model is an organizational design tool that helps connect vision and strategy with specific organizational characteristics and requirements. The plan includes specific steps and associated policy gaps that need to be addressed for each.
- Chapter 7, "Recommendations," briefly closes the report.
- Appendix A, "The Office of Homeland Security Statistics Logic Model," describes the model and findings from the LM workshop.
- Appendix B, "Overview of Relevant Authorities," describes the legal authorities for the office.
- Appendix C, "Candidate Personae and Scenarios for Stakeholder Engagement," outlines stakeholder persona examples and possible scenarios for stakeholder engagement.
- Appendix D, "The McKinsey 7-S Factors," describes the characteristics of the McKinsey 7-S LM.
- Appendix E presents the interview protocols we used with FSA and DHS representatives.

Overall, the report answers the why, what, and how questions about standing up OHSS. Although this study and implementation guidance are specific to OHSS, the background information, research questions and methods, and areas of focus for implementation will be of use to the launch of any future FSA.

# CHAPTER 2

# Background

## U.S. Statistical Agencies and Affiliates

### History

The U.S. government has long conducted statistical activities; indeed, the 1790 census was mandated by the Constitution (although the initial census was conducted by U.S. marshals). In 1884, Congress established the Bureau of Labor, the forerunner of the U.S. Bureau of Labor Statistics (BLS), as a separate agency; in 1902, Congress established the U.S. Census Bureau as a permanent agency.[1] However, statistical agencies and units were not recognized until a June 1997 OMB order, "Order Providing for the Confidentiality of Statistical Information."[2] At that time, 12 statistical agencies and units were subject to the order.[3]

In 2002, CIPSEA gave OMB the authority to recognize an agency or unit as a statistical agency or unit. This allowed RSAUs to collect data under a pledge of confidentiality that ensures that these data would be used only for statistical purposes. As of summer 2024, there are 13 FSAs and three statistical units, for a total of 16 RSAUs, although other statistical units that are not so recognized are permitted to collect data under this pledge as well. In addition, RSAUs have had to share confidential data. One example is the National Center for Education Statistics (NCES), a CIPSEA-designated agency but one that cannot use the pledge of confidentiality for certain collections it cannot prevent from being used for nonstatistical purposes under the Uniting and Strengthening America by Providing Appropriate Tools Required to Intercept and Obstruct Terrorism (USA PATRIOT) Act of 2001.[4] Title III of the Evidence Act reauthorized the confidentiality terms (with USA PATRIOT Act restrictions) in what is referred to as *CIPSEA 2018* and codified the four fundamental responsibilities of FSAs:

- Produce and disseminate relevant and timely statistical information.
- Conduct credible and accurate statistical activities.
- Conduct objective statistical activities.
- Protect the trust of information providers by ensuring the confidentiality and exclusive statistical use of their responses.

---

1 CNSTAT, 2021.

2 Office of Information and Regulatory Affairs (OIRA), OMB, Executive Office of the President, "Order Providing for the Confidentiality of Statistical Information," *Federal Register*, Vol. 62, No. 124, June 27, 1997 (final order).

3 OMB, "Fundamental Responsibilities of Recognized Statistical Agencies and Units," *Federal Register*, Vol. 88, No. 159, August 18, 2023 (notice of proposed rulemaking).

4 Public Law 107-56, Uniting and Strengthening America by Providing Appropriate Tools Required to Intercept and Obstruct Terrorism (USA PATRIOT) Act of 2001, October 26, 2001. We thank peer reviewer and former chief statistician of the United States (CSOTUS) Nancy Potok for this caveat.

CIPSEA 2018 also required OMB to develop guidance on the requirements and process for a PSA to obtain OMB recognition. As of this writing, that guidance is still forthcoming. However, OMB has noted that, "at minimum, agencies and units seeking this designation, along with their parent agencies, will be required to demonstrate a commitment to upholding the requirements in these regulations," in reference to requirements proposed in "Fundamental Responsibilities of Recognized Statistical Agencies and Units," commonly called the *Trust Regulation*.[5]

## Role

The United States has a decentralized FSS, in which the responsibility for producing official statistics for public use is spread across several agencies and organizational units in the executive branch.[6] The United States has 13 PSAs at the time of this writing and three RSAUs (Table 2.1); OHSS will be the 14th PSA. Besides the PSAs and units, more than 90 additional agencies and units are engaged in statistical activities; until recently, the Office of Immigration Statistics (OIS) fell into this latter category.[7]

PSAs and units are defined in law, most recently in the Foundations for Evidence-Based Policymaking Act of 2018, as "an agency or organizational unit of the executive branch whose activities are predominantly the collection, compilation, processing, or analysis of information for statistical purposes . . . ."[8] As OMB has stated,[9] "The public, businesses, and governments rely on the Federal statistical data produced by the Federal Government's statistical agencies, units, and programs to make informed decisions."

OIRA, part of OMB, coordinates the FSS.[10] OIRA's Statistical and Science Policy (SSP) Office, headed by CSOTUS, establishes statistical policies and standards, identifies priorities for improving programs, evaluates statistical agency budgets, reviews and approves information collections, and coordinates U.S. participation in international statistical activities.

In addition to leading the SSP Office, CSOTUS chairs the Interagency Council on Statistical Policy (ICSP), the membership of which is the heads of the 13 PSAs, the three RSAUs, and 24 SOs.[11] The ICSP, which OMB created in the 1980s and was authorized in statute in 1995, allows communication and collaboration across and sets strategic goals for the FSS (Table 2.2).[12]

[5] OMB, 2023.

[6] CNSTAT, 2021.

[7] Advisory Committee on Data for Evidence Building, Bureau of Economic Analysis (BEA), U.S. Department of Commerce, "The U.S. Federal Statistical System," briefing slides, January 22, 2021.

[8] U.S. Code, Title 44, Coordination of Federal Information Policy; Subchapter III, Confidential Information Protection and Statistical Efficiency; Section 3561, Definitions; Paragraph 11, Statistical Agency or Unit, as added by CIPSEA 2018, § 302, Confidential Information Protection and Statistical Efficiency.

[9] OMB, Executive Office of the President, *Statistical Programs of the United States Government: Fiscal Years 2021/2022*, February 2024, p. 2.

[10] OMB, 2024.

[11] Eleven of the heads of the 13 PSAs are also their agencies' SOs, so the total membership of the ICSP is 29, plus the chair. Two departments (the U.S. Department of Agriculture and the U.S. Department of Commerce) have multiple PSAs. The heads of the RSAUs were added to the ICSP in FY 2024 (ICSP, "Charter of the Interagency Council on Statistical Policy Subcommittee on Statistical Official Roles and Responsibilities," approved and adopted February 7, 2024).

[12] Paperwork Reduction Act of 1995 (44 U.S.C. Chapter 35); CNSTAT, 2021.

**TABLE 2.1**
**Principal Statistical Agencies and Recognized Statistical Units**

| Entity | Department or Parent Entity | Year Established |
|---|---|---|
| **PSA** | | |
| BEA | U.S. Department of Commerce | 1820 |
| NASS | U.S. Department of Agriculture | 1862 |
| NCES | U.S. Department of Education | 1867 |
| BLS | U.S. Department of Labor | 1884 |
| U.S. Census Bureau | U.S. Department of Commerce | 1902 |
| NCHS | U.S. Department of Health and Human Services | 1902 |
| SOI | U.S. Department of the Treasury | 1913 |
| ERS | U.S. Department of Agriculture | 1920 |
| ORES | Social Security Administration | 1935 |
| NCSES | U.S. National Science Foundation | 1950 |
| EIA | U.S. Department of Energy | 1977 |
| BJS | DOJ | 1979 |
| BTS | U.S. Department of Transportation | 1991 |
| **RSAU** | | |
| National Animal Health Monitoring System | U.S. Department of Agriculture | 1983 |
| Microeconomic Surveys | Federal Reserve System | 2009 |
| Center for Behavioral Health Statistics and Quality | U.S. Department of Health and Human Services | 2016 |

SOURCE: Features information from CNSTAT, 2021.

NOTE: BJS = Bureau of Justice Statistics; BTS = Bureau of Transportation Statistics; DOJ = U.S. Department of Justice; EIA = U.S. Energy Information Administration; ERS = Economic Research Service; NASS = National Agricultural Statistics Service; NCHS = National Center for Health Statistics; NCSES = National Center for Science and Engineering Statistics; ORES = Office of Research, Evaluation, and Statistics; SOI = Statistics of Income.

## Type of Statistical Agencies and Offices

Although PSAs share the same purpose and responsibilities, they vary in size, resources, and foci, among other features. Together, the U.S. Census Bureau and BLS accounted for more than half of the funding requested for PSAs in FY 2022 (excluding the funding to support the decennial census).[13] The Census Bureau employed 7,377 full-time staff in 2022, of whom 2,252 were statisticians and 117 were economists. In contrast, each of five smaller PSAs—BJS, BTS, NCES, NCSES, and ORES—employed fewer than 100 full-time staff, as shown in Table 2.3.

Ultimately, all PSAs are responsible to the U.S. public. However, because of their divergent foci, PSAs vary in their stakeholders. For example, in its mission statement, NASS specifically mentions "American farmers and ranchers" and "rural communities."[14] Similarly, BEA mentions businesses as important stakehold-

[13] OMB, 2024.

[14] NASS, U.S. Department of Agriculture, "About NASS," webpage, last modified May 4, 2018.

TABLE 2.2

**Members of the Interagency Council on Statistical Policy**

| Department or Parent Agency | PSA or RSAU | Member Type | | |
|---|---|---|---|---|
| | | PSA Head | SO | Chair |
| Board of Directors of the Federal Reserve System | Microeconomics Surveys | x | | |
| U.S. Department of Agriculture | ERS | x | | |
| | NASS | x | x | |
| | National Animal Health Monitoring System | x | | |
| U.S. Department of Commerce | BEA | x | x | |
| | U.S. Census Bureau | x | | |
| U.S. Department of Defense | | | x | |
| U.S. Department of Education | NCES | x | x | |
| U.S. Department of Energy | EIA | x | x | |
| U.S. Department of Health and Human Services | Center for Behavioral Health Statistics and Quality | x | | |
| | NCHS | x | x | |
| DHS | | | x | |
| U.S. Department of Housing and Urban Development | | | x | |
| DOJ | BJS | x | x | |
| U.S. Department of Labor | BLS | x | x | |
| U.S. Department of State | | | x | |
| U.S. Department of the Interior | | | x | |
| U.S. Department of the Treasury | SOI | x | x | |
| U.S. Department of Transportation | BTS | x | x | |
| U.S. Department of Veterans Affairs | | | x | |
| U.S. Environmental Protection Agency | | | x | |
| U.S. General Services Administration | | | x | |
| National Aeronautics and Space Administration | | | x | |
| U.S. National Science Foundation | NCSES | x | x | |
| U.S. Nuclear Regulatory Commission | | | x | |
| OMB | Office of the Chief Statistician | | | x |
| U.S. Office of Personnel Management | | | x | |
| U.S. Small Business Administration | | | x | |
| Social Security Administration | ORES | x | x | |
| U.S. Agency for International Development | | | x | |

SOURCE: Features information from StatsPolicy, undated

NOTE: A cell might be empty because the entity has an SO and agency-level activities but is not an OMB RSAU or PSA.

TABLE 2.3

**Numbers of Federal Principal Statistical Agency Staff Members in Fiscal Year 2022**

| PSA | Statisticians | Economists | Research Scientists | Other Statistical Personnel |
|---|---|---|---|---|
| U.S. Census Bureau | 2,252 | 117 | | |
| BEA | 8 | 284 | | 51 |
| BJS | 33 | | | |
| BLS | 165 | 1,169 | 10 | 970 |
| BTS | 24 | 15 | | 41 |
| ERS | 3 | 248 | | 3 |
| EIA | 84 | 84 | 66 | 10 |
| NASS | 591 | | 1 | |
| NCES | 55 | 1 | | |
| NCHS | 168 | | 87 | |
| NCSES | 25 | 3 | | 14 |
| ORES | 2 | 17 | 17 | 32 |
| SOI | 21 | 42 | | 1 |

SOURCE: Features information from OMB, 2024, Appendix Table 3, "Staffing Levels by Principal Statistical Agency or Unit."

ers.[15] Many PSAs engage with their stakeholders directly through advisory committees (ACs) and annual meetings.

PSAs also differ somewhat in their actual work, in terms of both data collection and types of statistical products. Historically, PSAs have gathered data primarily through surveys.[16] These include surveys of the public, such as the Census Bureau's American Community Survey, as well as surveys of select populations, such as NASS's dairy-product survey, which includes "cheese plants, butter plants, ice cream plants, and other facilities that commercially produce manufactured dairy products."[17] These also include surveys of state and local governments. For example, for its Annual Survey of Jails, BJS surveys a sample of approximately 950 local jails each year, and NCES's Common Core of Data is an annual collection from state education departments.

Although many statistical agencies have used surveys as their main method of data collection, PSAs are increasingly using administrative data, which are data collected by federal, state, and local government agencies for programmatic and regulatory purposes (although the FSS uses administrative data far less than European national statistical programs do).[18] For example, data assets for SOI, compiled by the Internal Rev-

[15] BEA, U.S. Department of Commerce, "Who We Are," webpage, last modified September 8, 2023.

[16] Notable exceptions include the Internal Revenue Service's SOI, ORES in the Social Security Administration, and BEA at the U.S. Department of Commerce.

[17] NASS, U.S. Department of Agriculture, "Surveys," webpage, last modified April 17, 2024.

[18] Panel on Improving Federal Statistics for Policy and Social Science Research Using Multiple Data Sources and State-of-the-Art Estimation Methods; Committee on National Statistics; Division of Behavioral and Social Sciences and Education; National Academies of Sciences, Engineering, and Medicine, *Innovations in Federal Statistics: Combining Data Sources While Protecting Privacy*, National Academies Press, 2017.

enue Service at the U.S. Department of the Treasury, stem primarily from federal income tax records.[19] In 2014, OMB issued "Guidance for Providing and Using Administrative Data for Statistical Purposes."[20] This memorandum, OMB M-14-06, encourages increased use of administrative data for statistical purposes, as well as increased documentation of administrative data. PSAs are also considering increasing the use of private data, which private-sector enterprises collect and PSAs purchase or otherwise acquire.

Finally, some statistical products are not raw survey data but analytics using data gathered by other PSAs. For example, BEA produces a variety of estimates, including gross domestic product, using data gathered by other PSAs, particularly the Census Bureau and BLS, as well as other federal data and data from private industry.

## Advisory Committees

Since 1972, CNSTAT at the National Academies of Sciences, Engineering, and Medicine has provided independent review of federal statistical activities.[21]

For the FSS, two committees advise multiple PSAs:

- FCSM advises the chief statistician and the ICSP on methodological and statistical issues related to federal data.[22] CSOTUS appoints the FSCM chair; the other members are career federal employees selected by OMB.
- The Federal Economics Statistics AC advises the directors of BEA and the Census Bureau, as well as the commissioner of BLS, on matters related to federal economic statistics.[23] This AC consists of approximately 16 members who are appointed by the Under Secretary for Economic Affairs at the U.S. Department of Commerce; the members should be professionals in appropriate disciplines from the public sector, academia, and the private sector.[24]

In addition to the cross-agency ACs, many statistical committees have their own ACs:

- BEA's AC consists of approximately 15 members from business, academia, research, government, and international organizations with expertise in economics, statistics, and accounting.[25]
- BLS sponsors two advisory groups, both of which have academics and experts from the private sector among their members:
  - The Technical AC advises the commissioner of labor statistics on statistical methodology and other technical matters.[26]

---

19 In addition to tax data, SOI has obtained access to datasets from the Census Bureau. These resulting data remain protected by the U.S. Census Bureau's requirement of confidentiality contained in U.S. Code, Title 13, Census.

20 Sylvia M. Burwell, director, OMB, Executive Office of the President, "Guidance for Providing and Using Administrative Data for Statistical Purposes," memorandum for the heads of executive departments and agencies, Memorandum M-14-06, February 14, 2014.

21 CNSTAT, 2021.

22 StatsPolicy, "About Us," webpage, undated.

23 StatsPolicy, undated

24 Federal Economic Statistics Advisory Committee, Office of the Under Secretary for Economic Affairs, U.S. Department of Commerce, *Charter*, September 27, 2022.

25 Bureau of Economic Analysis Advisory Committee, BEA, U.S. Department of Commerce, *Charter*, June 4, 2023.

26 BLS, U.S. Department of Labor, "Technical Advisory Committee Charter," October 4, 2022a.

  - The Data Users AC provides feedback on use and dissemination of BLS statistics, as well as on its published reports.[27]
- The Census Bureau has three ACs:
  - The National AC on Racial, Ethnic and Other Populations considers a variety of topics, including hard-to-reach populations and race and ethnicity.[28]
  - The Census Scientific AC advises the director on scientific developments in relevant areas, including survey methodology.[29]
  - The 2030 Census AC will review and provide feedback on 2030 census plans.[30]

Several PSAs, including BJS, do not currently maintain ACs. The Advisory Council on Transportation Statistics was created when BTS was established, for example, but it was terminated in 2018.[31] However, certain agencies fall under ACs operated by their home departments.[32]

### Agencies Outside the Executive Branch

Outside the executive branch, the Congressional Budget Office, GAO, and the Federal Reserve Board conduct statistical activities. Finally, the Administrative Office of the U.S. Courts houses the statistical office for the judiciary.[33]

## Statistical Activities in the U.S. Department of Homeland Security

The Foundations for Evidence-Based Policymaking Act of 2018 requires federal agencies to appoint SOs to serve with chief data officers (CDOs) and evaluation officers to further evidence-based policymaking activities. The CDO is responsible for, among other things, data governance in the department and leads the Data Governance Council. The SO promulgates standards for departmental statistical data to ensure their reliability and validity. It also conducts and oversees statutory statistical data reporting, among other things. Statistical data and reporting help inform the department's learning agenda and other evidence-building activities, which are coordinated by the evaluation officer.

For statistical activities within DHS, we recommend a definition of *statistical purpose* for OHSS use. In researching this issue, we had occasion to attend the FCSM conference in late 2023—and developed an understanding that the overall definition of *statistical purpose* is not set in stone across the FSS.

---

[27] BLS, U.S. Department of Labor, "Data Users Advisory Committee Charter," October 28, 2022b.

[28] U.S. Census Bureau, U.S. Department of Commerce, "2030 Census Advisory Committee (2030 CAC)," webpage, last revised October 17, 2023.

[29] U.S. Census Bureau, 2023.

[30] U.S. Census Bureau, 2023.

[31] BTS, U.S. Department of Transportation, "Advisory Council on Transportation Statistics," webpage, September 10, 2015.

[32] NCSES is part of the Directorate for Social, Behavioral and Economic Sciences, which has an advisory committee to advise NCSES as part of its duties. NCHS has a Board of Scientific Counselors. NCES has a National Board for Education Sciences that advises its parent, the Institute of Education Sciences (we thank peer reviewer Nancy Potok for this insight).

[33] Administrative Office of the U.S. Courts, "Statistics and Reports," webpage, undated.

## What Is Meant by "Statistical Purposes"?

There is no universally accepted definition for *statistical data*, or what would distinguish a data use as having a statistical purpose. Most definitions emphasize what these data are not: Statistical purposes are never intended to inform government actions involving specific individuals or groups. Having a formal and well-understood definition is essential to the FSS, as referenced in a draft trust regulation to be promulgated by OMB:

> Preamble: The Commission on Evidence-Based Policymaking emphasized that making data available for statistical purposes to advance evidence-building could place that data at **increased risk of being used for nonstatistical purposes** in ways that undermine the public's willingness to provide data to the Federal Statistical System, and thus recognized the need for "**strict structural and institutional separation between statistical and nonstatistical uses of data**," noting throughout its final report that a strong legal framework is needed to strengthen privacy and confidentiality protections for the data.[34]

However, in reviewing definitions provided at the FCSM conference in 2023, we found common elements across multiple definitions:[35]

- Data are kept confidential to protect the identities of people whose data are included in statistical products.
- Data may not be used by any government agency to target any person whose data are represented, including for any administrative, regulatory, law enforcement, adjudicatory, or other purpose that affects a right, privilege, or benefit of a particular identifiable participant.
- Data are intended to inform various stakeholders, including the public, academic researchers, and people involved in developing government policy.

The presentation also provided a useful history of statistical data use, including descriptions of infamous episodes in which data collected for statistical purposes were used for operational purposes. The Second War Powers Act of 1942 rescinded the Census Bureau's promises of confidentiality to provide the U.S. Secret Service with lists of every person of Japanese descent in Washington, D.C.[36]

The presenters also noted so-called *gray-area* characterizations of historical actions:

- In 1940, the U.S. Census Bureau lent its staff and expertise to the Immigration and Naturalization Service.
- Tract- and block-level tabulations were provided of Japanese, German, and Italian Americans (1942–1943).
- Custom tabulations were developed for DHS of Arab American households by country of origin at the ZIP Code level (2002–2003).

---

[34] Bob Sivinski, CSOTUS, "Statistical Purposes: United States and International Policy Framework," briefing presented at the Federal Committee on Statistical Methodology 2023 Research and Policy Conference, October 24, 2023, p. 9. Emphasis is in the original.

[35] This discussion is informed by notes we took during the presentation and the shared presentations following the conference. Also see Michael Hawes and Sallie Keller, "What Do We Mean by 'For Statistical Purposes Only'?" Federal Committee on Statistical Methodology 2023 Research and Policy Conference, Session B-5, October 24, 2023.

[36] Public Law 77-507, an act to further expedite the prosecution of the war, March 27, 1942.

The researchers presenting at the FCSM conference argued for further clarification of terms, given the efforts to make statistics more usable by providing finer-grained, detailed data and integrating additional data sources. One approach being considered is to establish tiered access controls, restricting access to only approved purposes and uses. The researchers recommended that any future definition would need to include the following:[37]

- approaches to balance data usability and sharing trade-offs with the need to maintain a statistical purpose
- the need to implement controls and restrictions within a dynamic environment
- methods to manage the statistics effectively for their purpose and use
- establishing a functional separation vis-à-vis measurement priorities.

Several of the sources listed in Table 2.4 are privacy documents, which illustrates that statistical data should first protect study participants and other people from becoming identifiable within the statistical products.

## What Is the Definition of Data Used for U.S. Department of Homeland Security Statistical Purposes?

We recommend that OHSS define *data used for DHS statistical purposes* as **quantifiable representations (descriptions, estimations, or analyses) of anonymized data such that no individual can be identified, personally targeted, or otherwise have their rights infringed, nor benefits received, as a result of its dissemination.**

The definition aligns with the others provided by focusing on the intent of using the data, the "purpose" being limited to "statistical purposes" only. We suggest that the definition emphasize the intent of statistical information for DHS (e.g., to provide insights into such questions as the performance of specific government programs and the decision environment that informs policy development, to inform academic research on topics across DHS missions).

## Component Overview

We reviewed statistical activities conducted by operational DHS components, particularly focusing on those components that had not previously worked closely with OIS on immigration-related statistical analyses. To investigate DHS components' statistical activities, we searched open-source websites, component websites, and previous RAND research. We also interviewed SOs from eight operational components:

- U.S. Customs and Border Protection (CBP)
- the Cybersecurity and Infrastructure Security Agency (CISA)
- the Federal Emergency Management Agency (FEMA)
- the Federal Law Enforcement Training Centers (FLETCs)
- U.S. Immigration and Customs Enforcement (ICE)
- U.S. Citizenship and Immigration Services (USCIS)
- the U.S. Coast Guard (USCG)
- the U.S. Secret Service (USSS).

[37] Sallie Ann Keller and Michael B. Hawes, "Deciphering and Interpreting 'for Statistical Purposes,'" briefing presented at the Federal Committee on Statistical Methodology 2023 Research and Policy Conference, October 24, 2023.

**TABLE 2.4**
**Definitions of Statistical or Nonstatistical Purposes for Data Use**

| Definition | Source |
|---|---|
| **Statistical purpose** | |
| Statistical purpose (A) means the description, estimation, or analysis of the characteristics of groups, without identifying the individuals or organizational that comprise such groups; and (B) includes the development, implementation, or maintenance of methods, technical or administrative procedures, or information resources that support the purposes described in subparagraph (A). | CIPSEA, § 502, Definitions, Paragraph 9; U.S. Chief Information Officers Council, "2.11 Confidential Information Protection and Statistical Efficiency Act (2002): Information Technology Laws," webpage, undated-b |
| "The privacy of data providers, the confidentiality of the information they provide, its use only for statistical purposes, and the security of the data are absolutely guaranteed." | European Statistical System Committee, *European Statistics Code of Practice*, rev. ed. 2017, endorsed November 16, 2017, Principle 5, p. 11 |
| "Individual data collected by statistical agencies for statistical compilation, whether they refer to natural or legal persons, are to be strictly confidential and used exclusively for statistical purposes." | United Nations Statistics Division, "Principle 6: Confidentiality," Fundamental Principles of Official Statistics, A/RES/68/261, January 29, 2014, p. 2 |
| "**Protect the privacy of data providers** (including individuals, households, enterprises, administrations, and all levels of government), and guarantee by the confidentiality of the individual information provided . . . for statistical purposes only." | Organisation for Economic Co-operation and Development, "Recommendation of the Council on Good Statistical Practice," OECD/LEGAL/0417, adopted November 22, 2015, amended March 12, 2019, § II(4) (emphasis is in the original) |
| Functional separation is "[s]eparating the use of information about an individual for a research or statistical purpose from its use in arriving at an administrative or other decision about that individual." | Privacy Protection Study Commission, *Personal Privacy in an Information Society: The Report of the Privacy Protection Study Commission*, July 1977, p. 572 |
| Statistical purpose primarily "means the description, estimation, or analysis of the characteristics of groups, without identifying the individuals or organizations that comprise such groups . . . ." | 44 U.S.C. § 3561(12), Statistical Purpose, as added by CIPSEA 2018, § 302(a) |
| "Statistical activities, for purposes of this Memorandum, include activities typically characterized as research, evaluation, and analysis, as long as the focus of those activities is on reporting aggregate findings about a group." | Burwell, 2014, § III, Scope |
| **Nonstatistical purpose** | |
| Nonstatistical purpose "means the use of data in identifiable form for any purpose that is not a statistical purpose, including any administrative, regulatory, law enforcement, adjudicatory, or other purpose that affects the rights, privileges, or benefits of a particular identifiable respondent . . . ." | CIPSEA, § 502, Definitions, ¶ (5)(a); U.S. Chief Information Officers Council, undated-b |
| Nonstatistical purpose primarily "means the use of data in identifiable form for any purpose that is not a statistical purpose, including any administrative, regulatory, law enforcement, adjudicatory, or other purpose that affects the rights, privileges, or benefits of a particular identifiable respondent . . . ." | 44 U.S.C. § 3561(8), Nonstatistical Purpose, as added by CIPSEA 2018, § 302(a) |

Operational components varied substantially in their processing and release of statistical data, as shown in Figure 2.1. Although the USCG has made approximately 17 databases publicly available (e.g., boating accident statistics), the Transportation Security Administration (TSA) makes only one similar database available

FIGURE 2.1
**Number of Datasets Produced by U.S. Department of Homeland Security Operational Components**

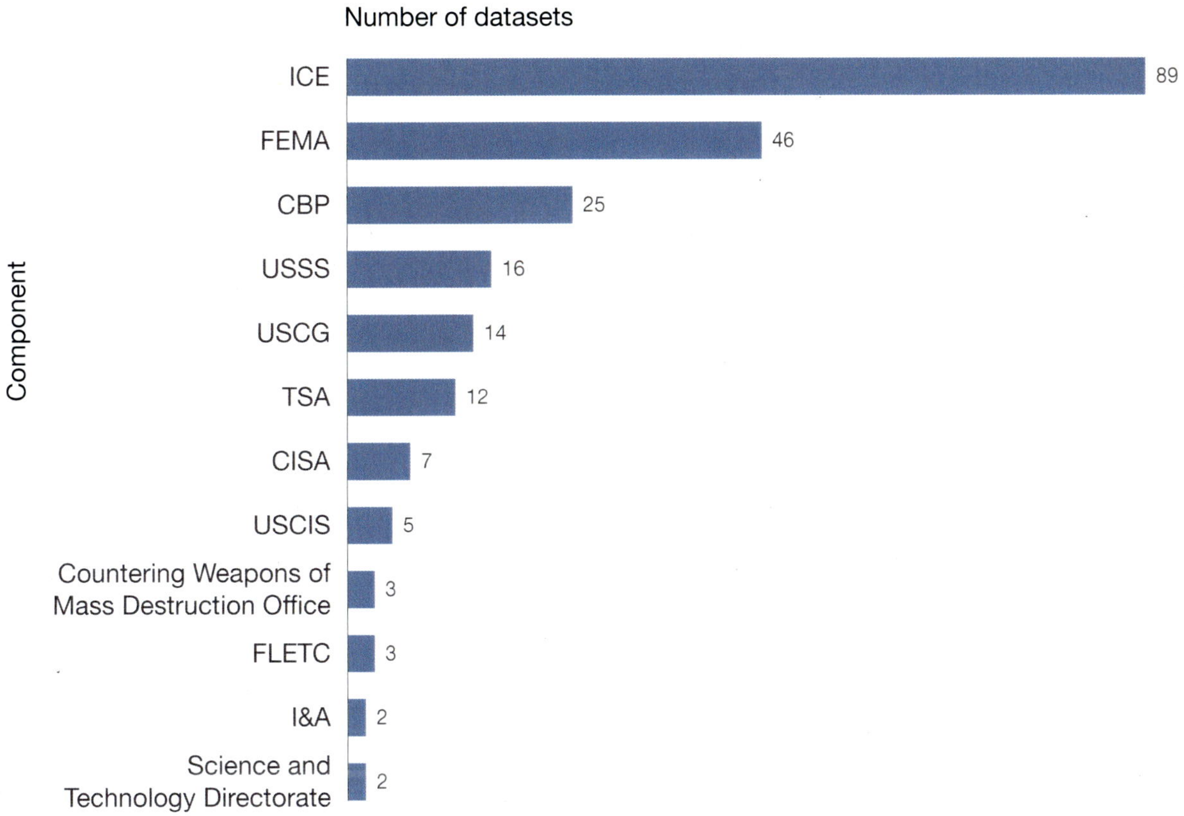


SOURCE: Features data from hundreds of publicly disclosed DHS datasets.
NOTE: I&A = Office of Intelligence and Analysis. The number of existing datasets does not indicate the data needs for each component—for example, some components might need data they are not currently reporting, and some datasets were created to respond to individual Freedom of Information Act (FOIA) (Public Law 89-487, an act to amend § 3 of the Administrative Procedure Act, Chapter 324, of the act of June 11, 1946, to clarify and protect the right of the public to information, July 4, 1966) requests.

(checkpoint travel numbers). Most data that components process seem to be administrative data, but FEMA conducts public surveys (e.g., the National Household Survey).[38]

Overall, many components' statistical reports and available public data appear to be one-time reports or responses to requests through FOIA, rather than consistently produced products. The number of FOIA requests to DHS rose substantially between 2008 and 2021, particularly for components working on human migration (see Figure 2.2). More problematic is that the complexity of FOIA requests has increased, resulting in longer response times (see Figure 2.3).

For 2017 to 2022, only CBP and OIS are listed in OMB reporting as having received direct funding for statistical programs; from 2018 to 2020, FEMA no longer conducted statistical activities that met reporting requirements.[39] In interviews, most component statistical staff described their offices as small. Statistical

[38] FEMA's National Household Survey is probability sampled: "FEMA administers the survey in English and Spanish via landline and mobile telephone to a random sampling of approximately 5,000 adult respondents" (FEMA, DHS, "National Household Survey," webpage, last updated December 22, 2023).

[39] OMB, Executive Office of the President, *Statistical Programs of the United States Government: Fiscal Years 2019/2020*, December 11, 2020; OMB, 2024. FEMA is listed as having received direct funding for statistical programs in Table 1b of the

**FIGURE 2.2**

**Freedom of Information Act Requests, by U.S. Department of Homeland Security Component, 2008–2021**

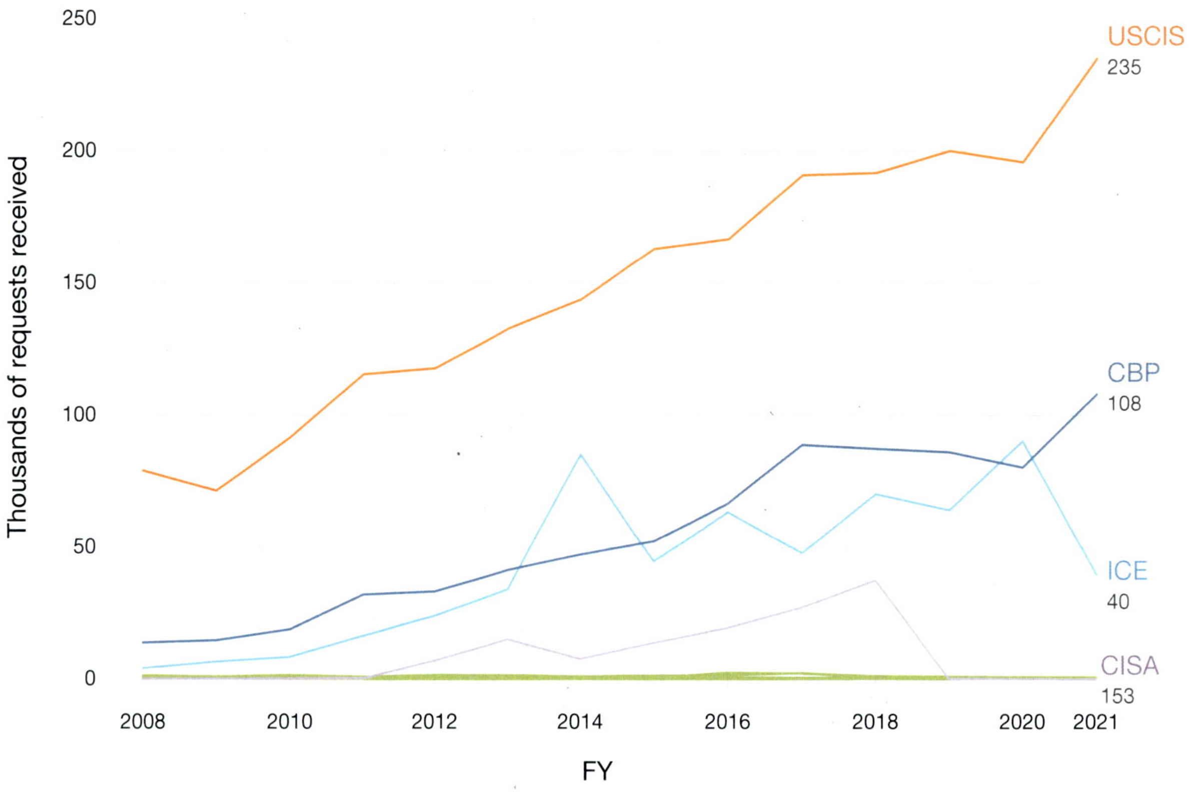


SOURCES: Features data from DHS, "FOIA Annual Reports," webpage, last updated March 25, 2024; and Office of Information Policy, DOJ, "Create an Annual Report," webpage, undated.

NOTE: Overlapping green lines at the bottom of the plot represent FEMA, FLETC, I&A, S&T, TSA, USCG, and USSS.

staff conduct analyses that support their components' multifarious activities. For example, FEMA staff are interested in enhancing predictive analyses to better focus emergency response, whereas FLETC staff would benefit from earlier access to personnel data to model training needs.

Given the diversity of DHS's statistical needs, activities, and burdens, component statistical staff in interviews indicated being cautiously optimistic about the promise of OHSS. Although some interviewees expressed concern about the potential for additional burdens (without additional resources), interviewees indicated particular interest in OHSS's role in standardizing variable definitions and analytical methodologies and in conducting research and issuing reports. Almost all interviewees indicated interest in collaborating on statistical activities more across DHS. When asked how OHSS could help support component statistical activities, some components' interviewees suggested that OHSS might help them interface more with other FSAs; other components expressed interest in access to data from other components to enhance their own analyses. Still other staff conveyed excitement about DHS viewing data as a mission-critical asset, especially in providing real-time decisionmaking support. Components' interviewees also mentioned increased access to expertise or specialized software as potential benefits of OHSS.

2019–2020 report for 2017 to 2019, but Table 1a states that FEMA no longer conducted statistical activities that met reporting requirements from 2018 to 2020.

**FIGURE 2.3**

**Freedom of Information Act Processing Times for U.S. Department of Homeland Security Simple and Complex Requests, 2008–2021**

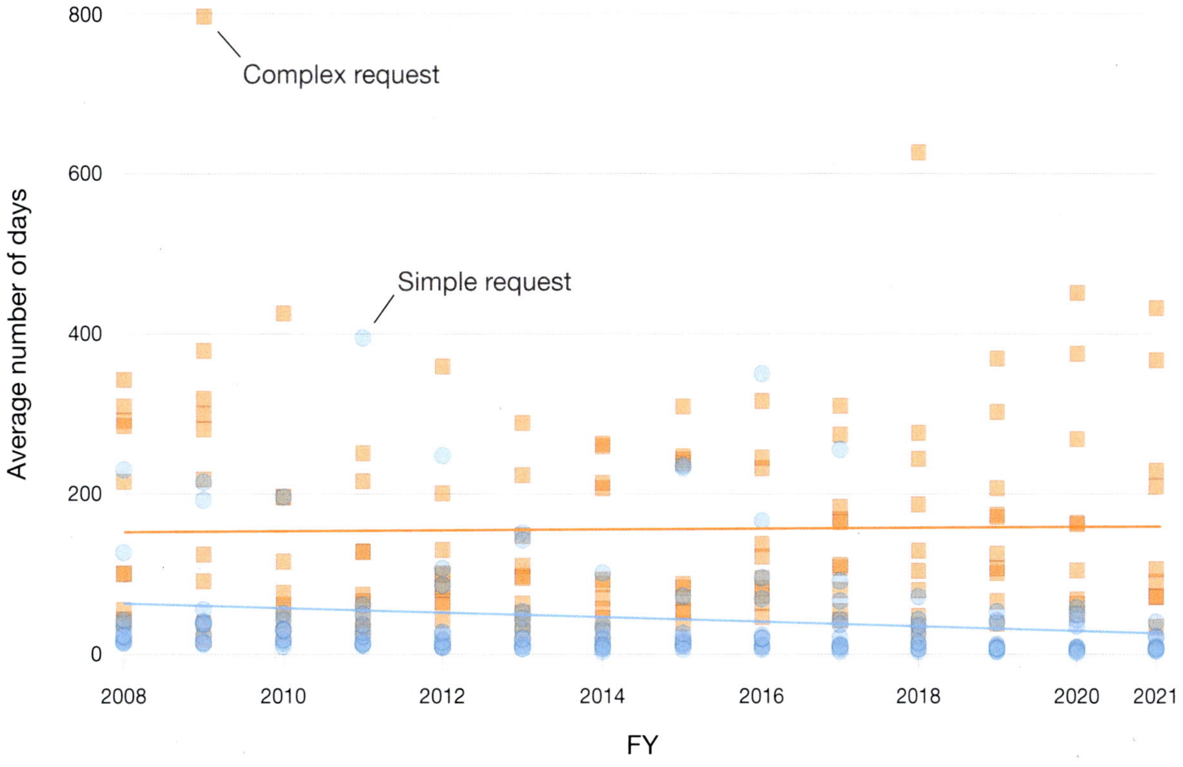


SOURCES: Features data from DHS, 2024, and Office of Information Policy, undated.

CHAPTER 3

# The Office of Homeland Security Statistics' Mission and Strategy

## Observations Influencing Mission and Strategy

In the course of this study to define OHSS, we observed several issues with which the newly created office will likely grapple. These observations emerged from literature, interviews with FSA principals, and presentations and on-site conversations during the FCSM 2023 Research and Policy Conference:

- There is an inherent tension for an FSA operating as the department statistical office while maintaining its independence from its parent agency, but there are also specific organizational behaviors and protocols that can provide that independence to maintain public trust.
- The FSS continues to grapple with balancing transparency of government data with protecting individual privacy. Much of the guidance on defining *statistical purpose* addresses the topic from a perspective of what it is not, emphasizing the need to obscure identifying data from statistical products.
- OHSS faces challenges that differ from those of existing RSAUs:
  - OHSS will not capture data directly but rather will develop statistical products informed by both administrative and operational data from among DHS components, crossing multiple domains aligned with the DHS mission set.
  - OHSS needs to coordinate with DHS component statistical offices; establish productive relationships; and, finally, develop guidance, standard operating procedures (SOPs), and protocols to scaffold these relationships and therefore ensure continued success under future leadership.
  - OHSS will provide both decision support and public reporting.

We considered these observations to draft a proposed mission statement and strategic pillars and objectives for OHSS. As GAO has previously noted, "strategies themselves are not endpoints, but rather starting points."[1] With this in mind, we sought to address areas necessary to provide OHSS with a foundation to effectively implement its statistical responsibilities for DHS while including aspirational elements designed to mature the organization as an RSAU. As we found during the project, a critical element to OHSS's success in DHS is developing effective partnerships with key stakeholders. Furthermore, the development of an official statistical system of record will aid the implementation of OHSS's statistical responsibilities and its RSAU mission. As OHSS implements its mission and strategic pillars and objectives, it might want to seek input from its key stakeholders to refine its strategy over time to ensure that its responsibilities are effectively met while maximizing its support of DHS's broader mission.

[1] Randell A. Yim, managing director, homeland security and justice issues, U.S. Government Accountability Office, *Combating Terrorism: Evaluation of Selected Characteristics in National Strategies Related to Terrorism*, statement before the Subcommittee on National Security, Emerging Threats, and International Relations; Committee on Government Reform; U.S. House of Representatives, GAO-04-408T, February 3, 2004, p. 12.

## Mission Statement

As detailed on OHSS's public-facing webpage, OHSS's mission is to **foster transparency and data-driven homeland security decisionmaking by analyzing and disseminating timely, objective DHS data and statistics.**

Recognizing the dual roles for OHSS, the director has established the following goals for the internal role of SO for DHS:[2]

> The core goals of OHSS are to:
>
> - Publish, maintain, and keep up to date enterprise-wide statistical standards;
> - Create objective, credible, accurate, relevant, timely, and authoritative statistical homeland security data products to increase transparency for the interagency, Congress, and the public and to support evidence-based policymaking and leadership decisions; and
> - Reduce the burden on DHS Components for statistical reporting.

In seeking designation as an RSAU, OHSS needs to consider additional goals that support the independent nature of an RSAU. Here we offer strategy pillars and objectives that align with both roles. The strategic pillars we describe in this chapter represent OHSS's overarching role as responsible for (1) establishing and maintain the DHS statistical system of record, (2) maturing departmental statistical activities across the components, and (3) functioning as an RSAU to join the 13 existing statistical agencies so designated by OMB.

In this chapter, we provide specific objectives to fulfill these roles and initiatives designed to satisfy these objectives. One foundational initiative that can be considered overarching and applicable to all pillars is to conduct a job analysis and develop competency assessment frameworks to establish OHSS's foundational staffing needs. This could involve the following:

- conducting an initial job analysis to identify foundational OHSS staffing needs, including the roles and responsibilities required to effectively carry out each OHSS activity
- developing comprehensive competency assessment frameworks for each role identified in the job analysis, including specific competencies, knowledge, skills, and abilities (KSAs) required to demonstrate success in each role.

## Pillar 1. Maintain the Official U.S. Department of Homeland Security Statistical System of Record

### Objective 1.1. Perform Chief Data Officer Responsibilities as Delegated for Agency Statistical Data

*Statistical data* is defined as "data for the purpose of describing or making estimates concerning the whole, or relevant groups or components within, the economy, society, or the natural environment."[3]

#### Initiative 1.1.1. Publish and Manage Enterprise Statistical Standards

Develop and maintain guidelines and protocols to ensure the accuracy of, consistency of, and relevant access to information for OHSS and components. Develop comprehensive standards and formalize a repeatable

[2] OHSS, DHS, "About OHSS," webpage, undated.

[3] 44 U.S.C. § 3561(10)(A).

process that enables OHSS to provide timely and relevant information to policymakers and other relevant stakeholders and promotes a transparent and accountable OHSS culture.

### Initiative 1.1.2. Develop, Publish, and Share an Office of Homeland Security Statistics Principle Memorandum That Defines and Provides Context for the Office's Dual Role

Formalize guidance and create shared situational awareness of OHSS's dual role (i.e., advancing DHS's statistical capacity and developing and disseminating statistical products independently of DHS influence or oversight) to assist with internal and external (e.g., public) clarification of function definitions and of responsibilities. Proactively share OHSS principles with internal and external stakeholders to simultaneously build trust among existing OHSS and component employees and stakeholders and to serve as a method of helping new hires better acculturate to the newly established organization, continuously relaying OHSS's organizational values and discrete mission objectives.

### Initiative 1.1.3. Develop, Publish, and Share Policy Documents Connecting Office of Homeland Security Statistics Standardization Authorities to Office Leadership Positions and Other Managerial-Level Responsibilities Across the Office

Map authorities to staff positions throughout OHSS to establish, solidify, and delineate between decision-making LOEs and congressional and departmental requirements. Identify synergies across positions.

### Initiative 1.1.4. Develop End-to-End Mapping of Office of Homeland Security Statistics Assets, Information and Material Flows, Decisionmaking Processes, and Key Decision Points to Allow Continual Organizational Learning and to Identify and Mitigate Cross-Cutting Challenges

Develop a process flow diagram that depicts organizational resource inputs, outputs, and outcomes (akin to the LM introduced earlier and discussed in more depth in Chapter 4) to help OHSS understand process efficiencies and inefficiencies that can highlight process gaps and inefficiencies. Include connectivity (information entry and exit points) to other systems, people (e.g., components), and processes that present a holistic view of OHSS's value to the statistical community.

### Initiative 1.1.5. Develop Specific and Measurable Lines of Effort That Outline the Office of Homeland Security Statistics' Role in Enabling Component Data Analysis and Reporting, and Establish Feedback Loops Between Relevant Stakeholders (Components) and Office Representatives That Maintain Consistent, Formalized Communication Networks

Ensure that data analysis and reporting activities are aligned with specific mission objectives and departmental goals. Construct LOEs that are specific, measurable, achievable, relevant, and time-bound (SMART) to facilitate the development of associated organizational metrics. Once they are complete, OHSS should strive to ensure that metrics continue to inform stakeholder needs on an ongoing basis.

### Initiative 1.1.6. Draft and Circulate Standard Operating Procedures for Data Requests to Ensure That Office of Homeland Security Statistics–Derived Data Are Managed and Disseminated in Accordance with Existing Legal Reporting Requirements

Ensure that OHSS data are stored, processed, and distributed in compliance with all legal requirements. Establish a formal, legal staff position that is responsible for ensuring compliance with emerging and future legislation that could restrict or otherwise prohibit the sharing of certain types of data with specific entities. This position would be responsible for monitoring and analyzing relevant laws and regulations to ensure that OHSS remains compliant and for developing and implementing procedures to protect sensitive information from unauthorized or accidental disclosure. Establish guidance and policy for responding to formal data requests, including FOIA and requests for information (RFIs). Consult with components and other established statistical agencies to ensure that OHSS-derived SOPs are consistent with community and legal standards. Provide training to all staff members, regardless of position, to ensure that everyone understands the SOPs.

## Objective 1.2. Partner with the Chief Data Officer on Their Management of Data Elements and Mechanisms

### Initiative 1.2.1. Develop Guidance to Assist the Office of Homeland Security Statistics in Partnering with the Chief Data Officer on the Management of Data Elements and Mechanisms That Meet 44 U.S.C. § 3520 Requirements

Per 44 U.S.C. § 3520, Chief Data Officers, the CDO is responsible for several functions, including the following:

- "lifecycle data management"
- coordinating with DHS officials who are "responsible for using, protecting, disseminating, and generating data to ensure that the data needs of the agency are met"
- managing "data assets of the agency, including the standardization of data format, sharing of data assets, and publication of data assets in accordance with applicable law"
- ensuring "that, to the extent practicable, agency data conforms with data management best practices"
- engaging "agency employees, the public, and contractors in using public data assets" and encouraging "collaborative approaches on improving data use."[4]

Develop guidance that conforms with and supports CDO activities to ensure adherence to congressional requirements as the organization matures.

### Initiative 1.2.2. Establish an Office of Homeland Security Statistics Advisory Committee to Provide Guidance and Support to the Office in Its Partnership with the Chief Data Officer

Establish a committee composed of statistical subject-matter experts (SMEs) and stakeholders to provide guidance and support to the OHSS/CDO partnership. The committee should serve as a forum for discussing and addressing issues related to data management, data quality, data governance, and data security and should consider providing recommendations (informal or formal) on best practices and strategies for improving data management practices through its engagements with the statistical stakeholder community.

## Objective 1.3. Partner with Component Statistical Officials to Understand Data-Sharing Needs and Constraints

### Initiative 1.3.1. Ensure That Component Voices Are Heard and Considered Through Formal Engagement and Feedback Mechanisms

Institutionalize formal mechanisms for cross-component collaboration (e.g., scheduled quarterly meetings, workshops, situational awareness trainings, surveys) to provide components with opportunities to provide feedback to OHSS and to gain additional insights and perspectives on analytical products and other offerings. Establish formal feedback loops with components to improve OHSS responsiveness.

[4] 44 U.S.C. § 3520, Authorization of Appropriations, (c), Functions.

### Initiative 1.3.2. Ensure That Office of Homeland Security Statistics and Components Understand Reporting Burdens

Establish a shared understanding of OHSS use and need for component data. Review existing resources and responsibilities, identify actions and activities that might share overlap that could be complemented through collaborative efforts, and plan for emerging efforts to ensure that DHS resources are used efficiently and effectively.

### Initiative 1.3.3. Develop Directives That Outline and Memorandums of Understanding That Provide for Rotational Assignments and Detailee Requirements for Component Statistical Staff to Better Understand the Mission and Operations of the Office of Homeland Security Statistics

In line with initiative 1.1.2, foster positive partnerships with component SOs, increase data-sharing, and identify needs and constraints as OHSS detailees cross-pollinate information gained from their rotational assignments. Develop memorandums of understanding (MOUs) that enact processes for data-sharing and reporting to facilitate partnerships with component SOs.

### Initiative 1.3.4. Develop Design Principles for the Desired Skills and Knowledge of Office of Homeland Security Statistics Staff

Promote a shared understanding of statistical standards and of OHSS's role in establishing and maintaining those standards, and help identify specific workforce skills and knowledge necessary to maintain OHSS operational activities.

### Initiative 1.3.5. Enact an Office of Homeland Security Statistics Quality Assurance and Quality Control Program to Ensure That Department Statistical Data Are of High Quality and Meet Established Standards

Develop a quality assurance (QA) and quality control (QC) program that includes SOPs for collecting, managing, and disseminating department statistical data. Provide a formalized (i.e., valid, reliable, and repeatable) approach to monitor and assess end-to-end data quality to help identify issues that could affect data quality or compliance with U.S. law.

### Initiative 1.3.6. Institute U.S. Department of Homeland Security–Compliant Data Security Tools to Support Office of Homeland Security Statistics Activities and Mission Requirements

Enhance data security and sensitive-information protection in line with U.S. law and DHS and CISA guidelines. Integrate data platforms and other analytical tools with security programs to adhere to DHS information-sharing standards and to demonstrate organizational commitment to data protection throughout the data life cycle (e.g., data ingestion, analysis, reporting).

## Objective 1.4. Support Evidence-Based Policymaking and Leadership Decisions

### Initiative 1.4.1. Produce and Disseminate Timely Statistical Information

In keeping with provisions in the Foundations for Evidence-Based Policymaking Act of 2018, conduct credible and accurate statistical activities that

- protect the trust of information providers by ensuring the confidentiality and exclusive statistical use of their responses

- use data acquired under a confidentiality pledge and for statistical purposes, in accordance with the pledge and for those specific purposes
- protect data by requiring specific disclosure statements for distribution
- develop a standardized process through which individuals and organizations can apply for access to the data assets.

## Pillar 2. Provide Statistical Data Services to Mature Departmental Statistical Activities

### Objective 2.1. Advise on Statistical Policy, Techniques, and Procedures

#### Initiative 2.1.1. Develop Policy Instructions for Independent Report Clearance, Review, Notification, and Release

Develop a process and accompanying policy for assessing statistical reporting and distribution to external stakeholders. Advise component SOs on good and emerging practices for statistical reporting.

#### Initiative 2.1.2. Develop a Directive That Outlines the Scope and Role of Component Review of Office of Homeland Security Statistics Products

Conduct a comprehensive review of existing OHSS products to determine areas for improvement and identify potential gaps in the current review process. Establish and define all roles and responsibilities of staff who will be involved in the product review process, including the review team leader, reviewers, and final-approval authority and objective approval criteria.

#### Initiative 2.1.3. Establish a Structure for Communicating Data Governance Approaches and Related Requirements for Component Data Governance

Identify key stakeholders involved in the development and implementation of the data governance structure. Define the purpose and objectives of the data governance structure, including the goals and outcomes to be achieved. Institutionalize a process for communicating the data governance framework to all relevant stakeholders, including component staff and cross-agency partners. Establish a system for monitoring and reporting on compliance with the data governance framework, including regular audits and assessments.

#### Initiative 2.1.4. Develop Guidance and Educational Aids Designed to Advance Statistical Data Literacy Throughout the U.S. Department of Homeland Security

Conduct a formal need assessment to identify gaps in statistical data literacy throughout DHS and determine the most-effective avenues for addressing identified gaps. Develop comprehensive guidance and educational aids (e.g., tailored training modules, workshops, webinars) to address identified gaps. Provide training and support to OHSS staff to ensure that they are equipped to effectively train external staff.

### Objective 2.2. Coordinate and Collaborate on Component Statistical Reporting Requirements

#### Initiative 2.2.1. Apply Knowledge Gained Through Stakeholder Communication to Enhance the Relevance of Office of Homeland Security Statistics Activities

Conduct stakeholder interviews, surveys, focus groups, and other engagements to glean insights that highlight stakeholder needs, preferences, expectations, and potential synergies with external organizations. Analyze stakeholder feedback to identify areas in which OHSS activities can be enhanced to better meet stakeholder needs and expectations.

#### Initiative 2.2.2. Enact Office of Homeland Security Statistics Processes for Data-Sharing and Reporting to Facilitate Partnerships with Component Statistical Officials

Map key data-sharing activities and relevant stakeholders to continuously identify, mitigate, and improve data-sharing needs and awareness.

#### Initiative 2.2.3. Develop Policy to Establish a Statistical Data Security Group Organized to Discuss, Inform, and Make Data Security Recommendations

Develop comprehensive policy for establishing a statistical data security group. Define the roles, functions, and responsibilities of each member of the statistical data security group. Establish a system for monitoring and reporting on compliance with security group–implemented policies.

### Objective 2.3. Provide Statistical Consulting Services to Components

#### Initiative 2.3.1. Develop Training Programs for Office of Homeland Security Statistics Staff to Provide Statistical Consulting Services to Components

Create training programs to equip staff with skills necessary to provide aid to DHS components. The training programs should include case studies and interactive sessions using plausible real-world examples to ensure effective knowledge transfer and retention.

#### Initiative 2.3.2. Develop a Methodology for Identifying and Mitigating Potential Biases in Data Inputs (e.g., Analysts), Data Outputs (Analysis), and Outcomes

Develop training and awareness programs that can foster a culture of continuous improvement and awareness around potential biases in data inputs, outputs, and outcomes, including recognition and rewards (i.e., incentives) for staff who demonstrate proficiency in identifying and mitigating potential data-based biases. Institute training programs that assist staff in identifying problematic biases within data.

## Pillar 3. Produce Independent Reports as a Recognized Statistical Agency or Unit

### Objective 3.1. Establish Independence from U.S. Department of Homeland Security Leadership (Pending Issuance of the Proposed Office of Management and Budget Trust Directive)

#### Initiative 3.1.1. Meet the Requirements to Become an Office of Management and Budget–Recognized Principal Statistical Agency

Develop strategic plans, policies, and instructions that conform with the statistical standards, data standards, and change management techniques contained in the delegation of authority from the DHS Under Secretary for Strategy, Policy, and Plans signed in FY 2023.[5]

---

[5] Silvers, 2023.

### Initiative 3.1.2. Follow Procedures Established in Office of Management and Budget Guidance on Compliance with the Confidential Information Protection and Statistical Efficiency Act

First, verify that "information supplied by individuals or organizations to an agency for statistical purposes under a pledge of confidentiality is used exclusively for statistical purposes."[6] Second, create data security protocols that "safeguard the confidentiality of individually identifiable information acquired under a pledge of confidentiality for statistical purposes by controlling access to, and uses made of, such information."[7] There are implications for record-sharing with other statistical activities. For example, at some point, OHSS might combine data with other statistical agencies that have collected data under an authority other than CIPSEA. These combined data should then be safeguarded according to relevant statute and appropriate data-sharing MOUs.

### Initiative 3.1.3. Prepare Annual Confidential Information Protection and Statistical Efficiency Act Reports to Office of Management and Budget in Accordance with Office of Management and Budget Guidelines for Compliance with the Confidential Information Protection and Statistical Efficiency Act

Ensure that CIPSEA reports provided to OMB adhere to OMB mandates. OMB requires that CIPSEA reports contain three key elements:

- the use of the CIPSEA pledge, such as the following:

  > Any Federal agency acquiring data under CIPSEA . . . shall report to OMB on an annual basis on those collections it has conducted under CIPSEA and affirm that the agency has followed the procedures in this guidance to ensure [that] the confidentiality of the information is protected.[8]

- description of the use of the CIPSEA agent provision (i.e., when or whether OHSS has designated agents who performed "exclusively statistical activities, including data collection, and are bound to the same legal requirements as agency employees for maintaining the confidentiality of the information")
- list of all data-sharing activities and practices to ensure adherence to OMB policy.

### Initiative 3.1.4. Mandate Annual Conflict-of-Interest Statements and Signatures for All Office of Homeland Security Statistics Staff

Create annual reporting procedures that require all staff members to submit annual conflict-of-interest statements. Create dedicated teams to review, identify, address, and mitigate potential conflict-of-interest reporting.

### Initiative 3.1.5. Conduct Regular, Periodic Reviews of Analytical Flows, Products, and Engagements with External Stakeholders

Develop dedicated workflows that routinely sample OHSS analytical products (inputs, outputs, and outcomes) and assess stakeholder relationships to ensure objectivity in OHSS actions and activities.

---

[6] U.S. Chief Information Officers Council, undated-b.

[7] U.S. Chief Information Officers Council, undated-b.

[8] OMB, Executive Office of the President, "Implementation Guidance for Title V of the E-Government Act, Confidential Information Protection and Statistical Efficiency Act of 2002 (CIPSEA)," *Federal Register*, Vol. 72, No. 115, June 15, 2007 (notice of decision). § VIII, Annual Reporting and Review Requirements, (A) Overview.

### Objective 3.2. Coordinate with Agency Stakeholders to Understand the Demand Signal for Regular and Occasional Reports

#### Initiative 3.2.1. Provide Regular and Ongoing Office of Homeland Security Statistics Workforce Development Opportunities for the U.S. Department of Homeland Security Statistics Community to Establish and Maintain the Office's Authority

Create a series of career personae that can illustrate potential career trajectories in OHSS and the DHS statistics community. Highlight available training and continuing education offerings, hypothetical advancement timelines, and connectivity to overall departmental goals and objectives.

### Objective 3.3. Advance the Public Understanding of the Office of Homeland Security Statistics as an Independent, Nonpartisan Resource

#### Initiative 3.3.1. Create Engagement Materials That Promote and Engage External Stakeholders Through Office of Homeland Security Statistics–Branded Products

Develop a strategic communication strategy that identifies (stratifies)

- potential stakeholder audiences
- targeted products to communicate OHSS actions and activities
- methods for engaging existing and new audiences.

#### Initiative 3.3.2. Conduct Regular (e.g., Quarterly) Office of Homeland Security Statistics–Public Brown-Bag Events That Relay Office Missions, Activities, and Unique Products

Implement in-person, virtual, or hybrid events that can relay OHSS impact, value, and efforts to interested and relevant OHSS stakeholders. Tailor delivery of the brown-bag events to internal and external audiences.

#### Initiative 3.3.3. Develop and Administer Surveys to Data User Communities to Help Identify and Mitigate Data User Community Wants and Needs and Help Anticipate Future Challenges

Consult with statistical agencies to understand key survey components, challenges, and enablers that can be operationalized to assist future OHSS LOEs. Leverage search and discovery platforms to identify data users for engagement to improve data access, quality, and relevance to their needs. This will include identifying users who are underutilizing or misusing OHSS data and engaging to increase awareness and address any issues.

#### Initiative 3.3.4. Develop and Institute a Knowledge Management System That Applies Knowledge Gained Through Stakeholder Communication to Enhance the Relevance of Office of Homeland Security Statistics Activities While Engaging with Public Statistical and Data User Communities

Develop and implement technology platforms that can capture, relay, and categorize stakeholder communications for process improvement and improve knowledge management functions during periods of staff turnover.

CHAPTER 4

# The Office of Homeland Security Statistics Logic Model

> The program logic model is defined as a picture of how your organization does its work—the theory and assumptions underlying the program. A program logic model links outcomes (both short- and long-term) with program activities/processes and the theoretical assumptions/principles of the program.[1]

In conjunction with OHSS stakeholders, we developed an LM for OHSS. An LM is a graphical, at-a-glance view of an organization or a program that defines what the organization or program does and why—what it seeks to accomplish. It is a visual narrative of how the organization or program takes in a series of inputs, uses those inputs in a series of major activities to create outputs, which, in turn, staff and stakeholders use to create positive outcomes. The LM is intended to be a tool to help OHSS in its strategic management; it serves as a point of reference to assess whether strategic and managerial goals, metrics, and candidates for investment are aligned with OHSS's core narrative (e.g., whether the proposed goals would lead to improvements in operations or outputs and, hence, improvements in desired outcomes).

This chapter first presents the LM we developed, and then provides the insights shared about specific LM elements during a fall 2023 workshop attended by DHS component stakeholders for OHSS.

## Data Collection and Logic Model Development

We developed an initial LM for OHSS through a review of a variety of sources. We reviewed laws and policy providing relevant purpose information for OHSS, with the Evidence Act being especially relevant. We also reviewed OHSS plans and materials, including orders, charters, and introductory briefings, as well as the proceedings of our interviews of OHSS's DHS and non-DHS stakeholders. We also reviewed guidance for FSAs—most notably, the National Academies' *Principles and Practices for a Federal Statistical Agency*.[2] To refine and validate the model, we held a daylong workshop in November 2023 with OHSS stakeholders and statistical SMEs. Appendix A provides the full treatment of the LM and processes used to create it, along with the proceedings of the workshop.

## The Office of Homeland Security Statistics Logic Model

The resulting LM is shown in Figure 4.1. Table 4.1 provides definitions for each of the major types of elements shown on the model.

---

[1] W. K. Kellogg Foundation, *Logic Model Development Guide*, updated January 2004, p. iii.

[2] CNSTAT, 2021.

**FIGURE 4.1**
**A Logic Model for the Office of Homeland Security Statistics**

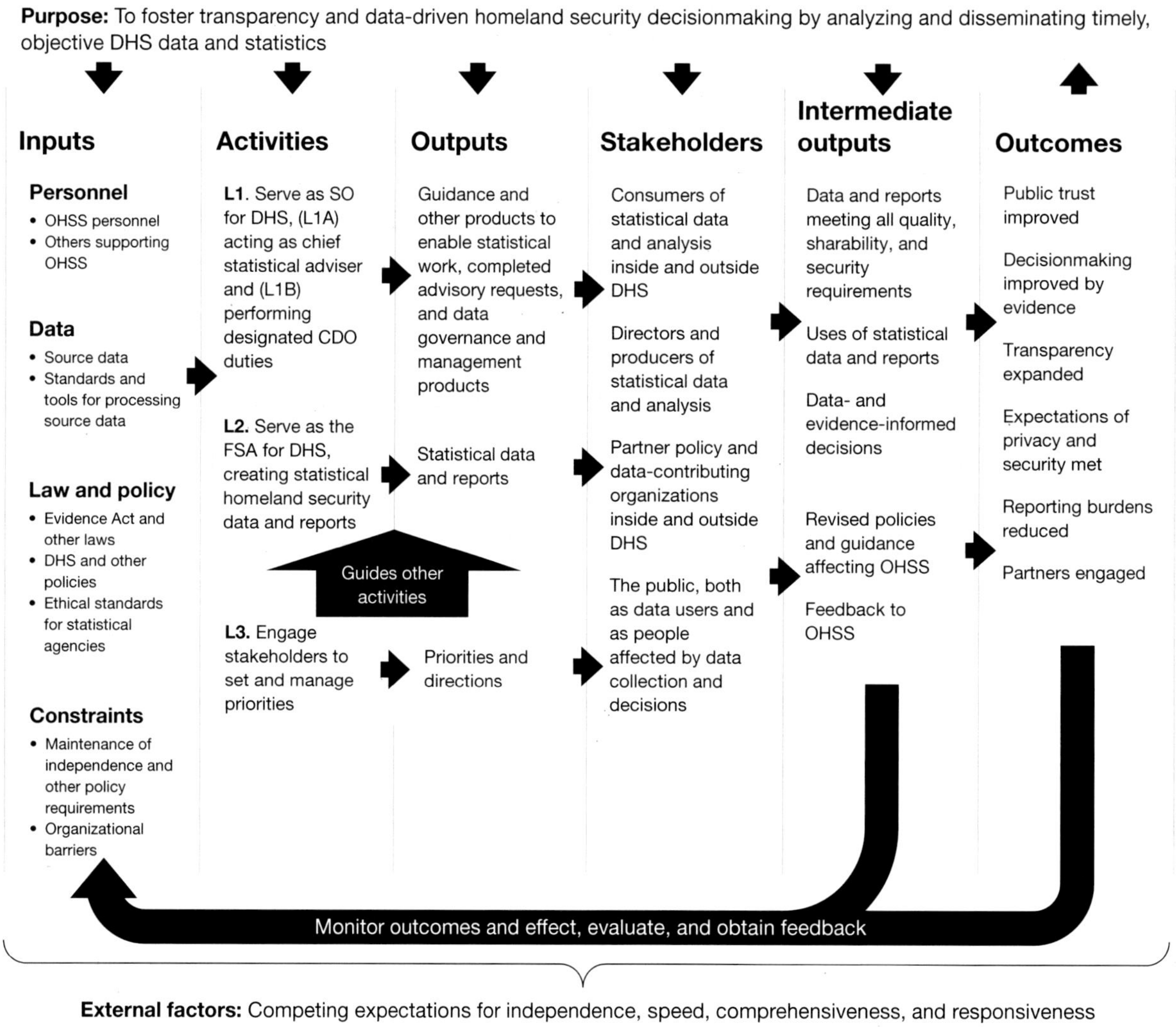


NOTE: The L numbers in parentheses indicate the portion of the logic model described in Table 4.2 later in this chapter.

## Purpose

The OHSS purpose statement was discussed during the workshop and reflects the observed consensus of the participants. It emphasizes the dual importance of OHSS supporting both improved decisionmaking and improved transparency (and public trust).

## Activities

From the workshop and preceding research, we determined that OHSS had three overarching activities:

- The first was to act as the SO for DHS. This is primarily an external outreach and coordination function; it includes serving as chief adviser on statistical matters and performing CDO duties to support the generation and use of statistical data.

**TABLE 4.1**
**Definitions of Elements Used in the Logic Model**

| Element | Definition |
|---|---|
| Purpose | One-sentence summary of what OHSS does |
| Input | A resource that goes into and guides activities |
| Activity | An action that a program undertakes, possibly with partners, to produce outputs |
| Output | A product (good or service) that an activity generates |
| Stakeholder | A person, group, or organization with a vested interest in OHSS inputs, activities, or outputs |
| Intermediate output | An action that a stakeholder (user of output) takes that depends on, transforms, or implements an output |
| Outcome | A change in knowledge, attitude, or behavior that occurs and a benefit that results directly or indirectly from an activity or output |

- The second was to serve as the de facto FSA for DHS. This activity includes preparing statistical homeland security datasets and reports.
- The third is to conduct the ongoing stakeholder outreach necessary to effectively guide the other two activities, resulting in updated priorities and directions. Outreach broadly needs to be provided to internal and external stakeholders, which are data users, producers, partners, and the public.

The resulting outputs closely relate to these three LOEs, including advisory guidance, data governance and data management products to facilitate proper production and use of data, statistical data and reports, and guiding priorities and direction from stakeholder feedback.

The strategic pillars and objectives introduced in Chapter 3 align with these LOEs, as shown in Table 4.2.

## Model Inputs

OHSS takes in as inputs personnel (both its own and those supporting its efforts), data (i.e., datasets and standards and tools for using the data, law and policy), and a series of constraints—most importantly, maintenance of independence and related policy requirements.

## Stakeholders and Their Outputs, Outcomes, and Feedback

The wide variety of stakeholders use these outputs in their own intermediate outputs: The stakeholders generate and use statistical reports and data and, perhaps most importantly, use data and reports to make decisions. They also provide feedback to OHSS.

Outcomes can be categorized as those directly related to improving data production and reporting processes (by reducing burdens on components), those related to decisionmaking, and those for improving trust with the public and with stakeholders.

More-detailed remarks about each phase of the LM are provided in the next section, from the proceedings of the LM workshop.

TABLE 4.2

## Alignment of Strategic Pillars and Objectives with the Logic Model's Lines of Effort

| LM LOE | Strategic Pillar | Objective | Source |
|---|---|---|---|
| L1. Serve as the SO for DHS. | 2. Provide statistical data services to mature departmental statistical activities. | | OHSS |
| L1A. Act as chief statistical adviser. | | 2.1. Advise on statistical policy, techniques, and procedures. | U.S. Code, Title 5, Government Organization and Employees; Part I, The Agencies Generally; Chapter 3, Powers; Subchapter II, Federal Evidence-Building Activities; Section 314, Statistical Expertise |
| | | 2.2. Reduce component statistical reporting requirements. | OHSS |
| | | 2.3. Provide statistical consulting services to components. | Us |
| L1B. Perform designated CDO functions. | | 1.1. Perform CDO responsibilities as delegated for agency statistical data. | 44 U.S.C. § 3520 |
| | | 1.2. Partner with the CDO on their management of data elements and mechanisms. | 44 U.S.C. § 3520 |
| L2. Serve as the FSA for DHS. | 1. Maintain the official DHS statistical systems of record | | OHSS |
| | | 1.4. Support evidence-based policymaking and leadership decisions | OHSS |
| | 3. Produce independent reports as an RSAU. | | OHSS |
| | | 3.1. Establish independence from DHS leadership | Pending OMB trust directive |

**Table 4.2—Continued**

| LM LOE | Strategic Pillar | Objective | Source |
|---|---|---|---|
| L3. Engage stakeholders. | 2. Provide statistical data services to mature the department's statistical activities. | | |
| | | 1.3. Partner with component SOs to understand data-sharing needs and constraints. | Us |
| | | 3.2. Coordinate with stakeholders to understand the demand signal for regular and occasional reports. | Us |
| | | 3.3. Advance the public understanding of OHSS as independent, apolitical resource. | Pending OMB trust directive |
| | | 3.4. Engage with public technical and data user communities. | Us |

## The Logic Model Workshop: Participant Remarks, by Phase

On November 1, 2023, we held a daylong workshop to

- obtain feedback from component-level SOs and similar officials to inform the operational LM and target operating model for the new OHSS, including its activities, outputs, and contributions to intended outcomes
- identify next steps for continuing to develop the OHSS models
- facilitate ongoing dialogue on the role of the new OHSS.

In the rest of this section, we relay information gleaned during this workshop toward LM refinement. For an expanded view of participant discussions (including the prompts we developed for discussion), see Appendix E.

### Program Inputs

Much of the workshop discussion about LM inputs focused on data sources, data standards, and authorities' distinctions. Workshop participants relayed that OHSS should differentiate between its organizational activities in the input phase, given that the OHSS efforts can support both internal and external stakeholders. This dual-support function in the input stage has created some obstacles to standing up OHSS, including branding and messaging about OHSS activities to other DHS components.

Some participants expressed concern about CDO and OHSS data standards, usage, and consumption that would need to be accounted for in the input stage. Some participants also noted that staff across DHS might continue to conflate SOs (i.e., external-facing authority) with the head of a statistical agency (i.e., inward-facing authority), and such conflation would complicate information-sharing agreements between OHSS and components. Participants suggested that clarifying (and codifying) organizational relationships, authority, and roles in the initial LM phase could help establish and maintain OHSS independence.

Participants also highlighted several unique challenges that should be addressed in the input stage to ensure an efficient and effective statistical data ecosystem in subsequent LM phases:

- First, OHSS will need to develop a prioritization mechanism to triage internal and external RFIs. Participants noted that the type (e.g., urgency) of RFI could cause analytical trade-offs between quality and timeliness because of a lack of staff in the output and outcome portions of the LM. One participant noted that OHSS did not have the capacity to respond to competing demands from DHS components and the public, which further compounded challenges in the input portion.
- Second, participants indicated that an existing lack of data-sharing agreements with components could lead to data-access constraints, having cascading effects across other LM phases. Several participants generally indicated that establishing component-level data liaisons could mitigate some of the challenges associated with data inputs.
- Third, participants signaled that OHSS will need to ensure that internal stakeholders understand key differences between operational and statistical data and associated standards to avoid misinterpretation and misapplication of data in subsequent LM phases.
- Fourth, many noted that OHSS's information technology (IT) platforms might not be equipped to facilitate required inputs because of existing information silos. Participants recommended that OHSS establish two separate IT infrastructures (i.e., one to access and process component data to produce a product and the other to serve as a repository to manage data standards and methodologies) to facilitate inputs required.

## Program Activities

Participant discussions on LM activities focused primarily on OHSS coordination with component statistical offices, and positioning OHSS as a "champion" for data-driven decisionmaking across DHS. Workshop participants also listed several other activities intended to achieve organizational objectives. Some key activities included

- drafting analytical standards (and making recommended changes to standards when required)
- performing statistical analysis and modeling (including statistical meta-analysis)
- informing DHS budget and policy development (e.g., DHS's resource allocation decision and its planning, programming, budgeting, and execution processes)
- improving policymaker decisionmaking through increased analysis and justification
- maintaining communication networks between OHSS, components, and stakeholders.

Participants also offered numerous metrics that could facilitate activity tracking and process refinement as OHSS matures. For example, many said that OHSS would need to develop core sets of metrics set against discrete report timelines to track organizational activities. Participants also suggested that using a reporting timeline could reduce the number of RFIs (e.g., Congress, academia), which could alleviate some capacity issues in the input portion of the LM.[3] One key challenge that surfaced during discussions was the develop-

[3] Some other metrics offered in the activity portion of the workshop included "response time, report quality, and urgency [priority] level addressed." Others suggested that the number of external organizations receiving reports, the number of OHSS website "visits," the "percentage of FOIA requests addressed versus received," the "data wanted versus percentage of data accessible" and the number of "on-time reporting" records or products could capture output metrics and outcome metrics for OHSS leadership.

ment of activity measures for stakeholder engagement and liaison functions (activities), said to be a challenge because of the sheer number of people who could benefit from OHSS analysis.

## Program Outputs

Much of the discussion on LM outputs focused on statistical report production, data standards and governance-material production, and coordinating enterprise standards functions across DHS headquarters and components. Participants indicated that standards for statistical data in the output portion of the LM must be consistent across DHS to ensure OHSS efficiency and effectiveness. Participants also debated OHSS's role in reporting, protecting, and providing access to statistical data. For example, some noted that, if the data were statistical data, existing DHS and OMB policies had already delegated those functions and responsibilities. However, participants noted that formalized SOPs were lacking for operational-level data throughout DHS. One participant noted that liaison functions in the output portion could facilitate increased coordination between component statistical offices to harmonize output results.[4] Other members acknowledged that organizational branding, communication, and transparency should play a prominent role across OHSS outputs. However, some participants emphasized that data disclosure practices can be a difficult topic for OHSS because some regulations prevent information dissemination to components (and the public).

## Stakeholder Activities

Workshop participants noted that OHSS serves diverse stakeholder populations, and numerous LOEs will be needed to cultivate, engage, and maintain stakeholder relationships. Participants listed external U.S. government departments and agencies (e.g., Congress; OMB; the National Security Council; the Domestic Policy Council; DOJ; the U.S. Department of Health and Human Services; federal, state, local, tribal, and territorial entities; and other FSAs and statistical offices), internal DHS stakeholders (e.g., the Office of the General Counsel, I&A, the Privacy Office), and public institutions (e.g., academia, media, foreign institutions) as key stakeholder groups. Participants noted that OHSS must formalize feedback loops in this part of the LM to ensure product relevance and consumer satisfaction, cultivate information-sharing relationships, and elicit information that can help OHSS continue to learn about stakeholder community needs.[5]

## Intermediate Outputs

Workshop participants suggested that the intermediate output portion of the LM should focus on OHSS analysis and modeling, informing decisionmaking based on data, developing budgets (and budget justifications), and eliciting component feedback. There was some debate over whether drafting statistical and operational standards represented an LM intermediate output or an outcome; this was not fully resolved during the workshop. Discussions also centered on what other FSAs provide to their organizational leadership and the need to foster a greater understanding of how stakeholders use OHSS products. Some sugges-

---

[4] One participant noted that OHSS would begin conducting "road shows" in FY 2024 to showcase mutual benefits between (1) component data streams and (2) OHSS products and outputs that could lead to the establishment of relationships with other FSAs.

[5] Workshop participants noted that, although OHSS has some interaction with existing stakeholders, such communication remains in a nascent stage (primarily as a means to informally keep in touch). Feedback loops can be especially important between OHSS, DHS components, and external stakeholders because components might not have situational awareness on DHS leadership priorities and therefore might not be able to "help OHSS help stakeholders, since we are not in all the meetings." Improved collaboration between OHSS, components, and stakeholders could also highlight duplicative efforts (data redundancies), once established.

tions included creating feedback loops or liaison positions. Additional factors for consideration included facilitating access to data sources, supporting evaluation office deliverables, and responding to congressional and media requests.

## Outcomes

The overarching themes for LM outcomes included building and maintaining public trust, establishing a reputation for independence, and improving DHS decisionmaking. Although it would be "difficult to measure," participants suggested that OHSS should strive to establish a reputation of independence and credibility that leads to improved decisionmaking and continuous U.S. government process improvement. This primary theme also affected the session exploring OHSS's organizational purpose. The original purpose statement presented to each group about OHSS's purpose read as follows: "Maximize data transparency and consistency, support data-driven decisionmaking, and improve efficiency of statistical reporting." Workshop participants revised this original purpose into the following statement: "OHSS will enable data-driven decisionmaking by maximizing data quality, transparency, and objectivity." Others suggested that OHSS should also serve as a "centralized data source that is approved by all stakeholders and serves as a centralized, secure repository for the public and researchers to access data" by using the AORTAS mnemonic: accurate, objective, relevant, timely, accessible statistics.

CHAPTER 5

# Stakeholder Engagement

OHSS seeks to become intentional in its analysis and dissemination of DHS statistical data. This requires understanding the various partner and customer types that will seek to engage with DHS data.

Per objective 3.2, we developed an approach for stakeholder engagement using personae and scenarios. A persona is an archetypal individual profile that represents the needs of a specific group (e.g., academic researcher, journalist, concerned citizen). A persona captures the user group's goals, expectations, motivations, and challenges faced in achieving their goals. Scenarios place these personae into specific situations to help researchers understand the users' likely journey as they navigate DHS statistical data and processes. The intent is to aid OHSS in understanding its partner and customer base in a manner than can be easily understood and communicated as the organization is established over time. Through this exercise, OHSS can come to appreciate stakeholder goals, challenges, and potential roadblocks that can be addressed through an engagement strategy.

The initial identification of stakeholders developed for the LM effort resulted in an extensive list of both internal and external stakeholders that was too long and diverse to effectively guide engagement decisions. Therefore, we reviewed popular market segmentation methods and used an a priori method based on characteristics common among them. Specifically, we defined stakeholder groups first by the nature of their power relationships with OHSS and their professional use or nonuse of OHSS products. We populated the segments with stakeholders from the original list, and we reviewed the resulting framework with OHSS and RAND personnel to collapse unused segments and gain concurrence that OHSS could treat the resulting clusters of relational combinations similarly. For each of the final five stakeholder segments, a persona was created with attributes that resulted in realistic and tailored fictional representatives of each segment.

## Identify Stakeholders

We identified the following list of OHSS stakeholders through an iterative process of nomination and refinement to establish groups with expected interactions with OHSS activities and products. Although U.S. citizens, foreign nationals, and refugees were also identified as groups represented in and affected by DHS statistical analysis and reports, other stakeholder groups on the list would likely act as intermediaries between those individuals and OHSS, thus becoming the primary stakeholder. During the workshop, some OHSS leaders did express a desire to include the perspectives of these groups in the future, even if not through traditional stakeholder engagement. The final stakeholder list was as follows:

- DHS leadership
- OMB OIRA SSP
- DHS Office of Strategy, Policy, and Plans (PLCY)
- DHS Office of the Chief Financial Officer (Program Analysis and Evaluation)
- DHS Office of the Chief Information Officer (OCIO)
- DHS component statistical offices

- other DHS offices
- SO Council support staff
- Congress
- federal, state, and local agencies
- foreign partners
- nongovernmental organizations (NGOs)
- private-sector businesses and professional associations
- any critical infrastructure sector that had DHS as its sector risk management agency (chemical; commercial facilities; communications; critical manufacturing; dams; emergency services; government services and facilities; IT; nuclear reactors, materials, and waste; and transportation systems)
- research organizations
- media organizations.

## Construct Stakeholder Groups

We defined OHSS's stakeholder groups primarily by their expected relationships with OHSS and included groups representing combinations of those relationships. We identified three types of stakeholder relationships as defining the array of expected interactions with OHSS activities and products:

- The **Command** relationship is one in which the stakeholder has a greater or lesser influence on what OHSS does, how it operates, what it produces, or who is involved.
- The **Collaborate** relationship is characterized by stakeholders with which OHSS has a bidirectional relationship for data-sharing, analytical approaches, and insight development.
- The **Consume** relationship assumes a broad use of OHSS products by various groups and organizations with their own goals and agendas, with the common factor being the process of requesting or receiving data.

Table 5.1 lists all seven possible relational combinations of the three identified relationship types without repetition.

## Collapse Unlikely or Undesired Stakeholder Constructs

Once we had identified OHSS's stakeholders and established the stakeholder relationship types, or constructs, the next step was to remove unnecessary constructs:

- One set of unnecessary constructs was determined after the identified stakeholders were grouped according to the construct categories; any constructs not containing any stakeholders were removed from the persona development process.
- The second group of unnecessary constructs were those that were undesired as a construct in the final persona group. A valid construct must be removed intentionally and with great care because doing so removes fidelity and could result in less-effective stakeholder management. All stakeholders that would be assigned to the undesired construct must be accounted for elsewhere in the constructs.

After discussion by each group, the removal of the command-only and collaborate-only constructs was independently validated by RAND SMEs and OHSS leaders. Table 5.2 shows the resulting groupings.

TABLE 5.1
**The Seven Possible Combinations of Stakeholder Relationship Types**

| | Stakeholder's Role | | |
|---|---|---|---|
| **Relationship Type** | **Direct** | **Collaborate** | **Consume** |
| Command only | Directs OHSS's work generally or specifically | — | — |
| Collaborate only | — | Collaborates on ongoing projects | — |
| Consume only | — | — | Consumes completed OHSS products |
| Command and collaborate | Directs OHSS's work | Collaborates on work and associated products | — |
| Command and consume | Directs OHSS's work | — | Consumes the resulting products |
| Collaborate and consume | — | Collaborates with OHSS on ongoing projects | Consumes the resulting products |
| Command, collaborate, and consume | Directs OHSS's work generally or specifically | Collaborates on ongoing projects | Consumes the resulting products |

TABLE 5.2
**Stakeholder Constructs**

| Stakeholder Construct | Stakeholder |
|---|---|
| Command only | None |
| Collaborate only | None |
| Consume only | • Federal, state, and local agencies<br>• NGOs<br>• Private-sector businesses and professional associations<br>• Critical infrastructure sectors that have DHS as their sector risk management agencies<br>• Foreign partners<br>• Media organizations |
| Command and collaborate | • OMB OIRA SSP<br>• DHS PLCY |
| Command and consume | • DHS leadership<br>• Congress |
| Collaborate and consume | • DHS component statistical offices<br>• Other DHS offices<br>• Research organizations<br>• SO Council support staff |
| Command, collaborate, and consume | • DHS Office of the Chief Financial Officer (Program Analysis and Evaluation)<br>• DHS OCIO |

## Enrich Stakeholder Constructs with Representative Personae

Once we arrived at a manageable set of stakeholder groupings, we were able to develop relatable and representative personae—designed to help identify and communicate the value proposition realized by stakeholders resulting from the relevant organizational change. This approach is referred to as *developing personae and scenarios*, a method derived from the design-thinking movement in the early 21st century. In discussing the innovations of Thomas Edison, for example, Tim Brown observed,

> Edison's approach was an early example of what is now called "design thinking"—a methodology that imbues the full spectrum of innovation activities with a human-centered design ethos. By this I mean that innovation is powered by a thorough understanding, through direct observation, of what people want and need in their lives and what they or dislike about the way particular products are made, packaged, marketed, sold, and supported.[1]

This focus on human-centered design, which includes understanding people's needs, has been applied outside the field of innovation research and is now often used in change management initiatives:[2]

> [People are] the most important focus area of change, since ultimately it is the people, primarily the employees of the enterprise, who are responsible for institutionalizing an organizational change. Talking of people, it is important to understand the cultural, geographical, and demographical diversity of employees within an enterprise. Beyond diversity, it is also important to understand the wide spectrum of information consumers (user personas), that exist in any enterprise, and their diverse analytical needs. Change management strategy need [sic] to be developed for each user persona so that they embrace new technologies and new ways of working.[3]

The use of personae and scenarios was suggested to the study team during our interviews with FSA SMEs; at least one existing FSA reportedly had used this method to better understand and connect with its information consumers and providers.

We developed a template to develop each construct into a fictional persona that represented an example of the type of person who might have such a relationship with OHSS and developed candidate personae and specific scenarios for consideration in future stakeholder engagement communications and collaboration. These candidate personae and scenarios are provided in Appendix C.

---

[1] Tim Brown, "Design Thinking," *Harvard Business Review*, June 2008.

[2] Prakash Sah, *Defining Enterprise Data and Analytics Strategy: Pragmatic Guidance on Defining Strategy Based on Successful Digital Transformation Experience of Multiple Fortune 500 and Other Global Companies*, Springer, 2022.

[3] Sah, 2022, p. 87.

CHAPTER 6

# The Implementation Plan

When establishing or altering an organization, the use of a target operating model is helpful for defining necessary tasks with some means of separating independent efforts into manageable elements for more-efficient implementation. The implementation of OHSS is, at its heart, a change management endeavor. The establishment of this new office under PLCY necessitates change across all DHS components. We used the McKinsey 7-S target operating model to identify the organizational scaffolding measures that need to be addressed for each aspect of the organization. For this implementation plan, we augmented the 7-S target operating model, where appropriate, by identifying critical questions that could be addressed with future policy directives—largely to identify how OHSS works across DHS component statistical activities. The policies associated with functioning as an RSAU under OMB are contained in OMB directives, including the proposed trust directive detailed in Appendix B.[1] The full raft of policies that will enable OHSS to function as the department statistical office are yet to be drafted.

## Target Operating Model

A review of the relevant literature reveals several change models, each with its own branches of descendants and variants. One of the more established, commonly used, and widely understood models of organizational change is the McKinsey 7-S framework.[2] This framework was first established in the late 1970s to address the question of why organizational performance could not be predicted based on an organization's structural components alone as it grew in both size and complexity. Consultants at McKinsey's Organizational Effectiveness practice identified six additional perspectives of the organization that played a role in sustaining successful change.[3] Moreover, they found that all seven were interrelated, influencing each other in addition to overall performance. As the model matured, the seven factors came to be listed as *shared values*, *skills*, *style*, *staff*, *structure*, *strategy*, and *systems*. Figure 6.1 emphasizes the interdependence of the various elements and the centrality of establishing and maintaining shared values.[4] This insight aligns with Philip Selznick's view that the role of leadership consists of instilling institutional values that eventually cause identification within

1 OMB, 2023.

2 Oya Zincir and Ayşegül Özbebek Tunç, "An Imagination of Organizations in the Future: Rethinking McKinsey's 7S Model," in Roman Batko and Anna Szopa, eds., *Strategic Imperatives and Core Competencies in the Era of Robotics and Artificial Intelligence*, IGI Global Publishing, 2017.

3 The practice is now the People and Organizational Performance practice (McKinsey and Company, "People and Organizational Performance," webpage, undated).

4 John Hayes, *The Theory and Practice of Change Management*, Palgrave Macmillan, 2014, p. 137.

**FIGURE 6.1**
**The McKinsey 7-S Framework**

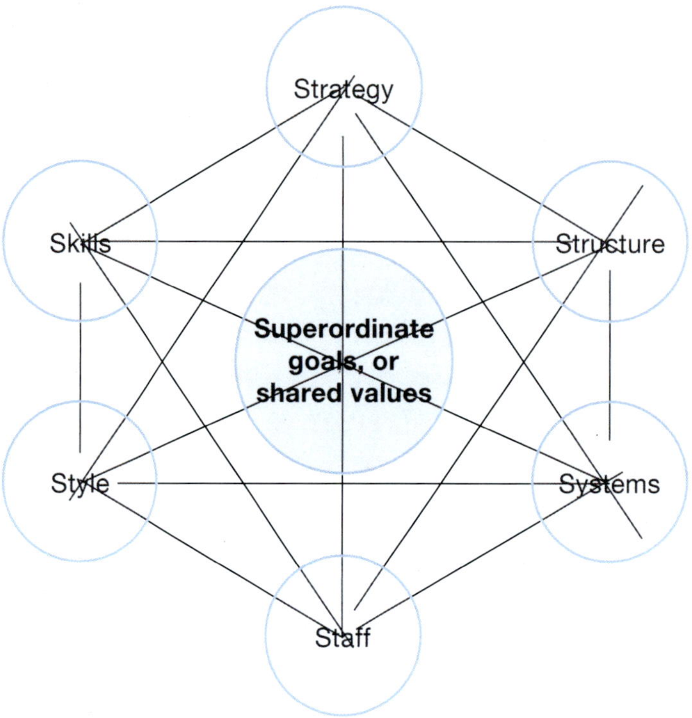


SOURCE: Adapted from Hayes, 2014, p 137.

the organization—a transcendence of individual self-interest in favor of perpetuating the firm.[5] We provide brief descriptions of how each factor is expressed:

- **Shared values** are the fundamental guiding principles and aspirations on which an organization is built. An organization's true values are often unwritten and notoriously difficult to quantify or evaluate directly, but every member will have an implicit understanding of what they are. Ultimately, an organization's shared values provide stability to an otherwise ever-changing system.
- **Skills** are an organization's capabilities, ensconced in its people and in their aggregation; in healthy organizations, the whole is greater than the sum of its parts. The skills that an organization needs change over time as the other 7-S factors change, so the ability to add needed capabilities and remove unnecessary ones is critical to organizational performance.
- **Style** is a direct reflection of an organization's culture and can be seen in how managers and leaders in the organization spend their time and attention. An organization's style is expressed in how the purpose of the organization is reflected in everyday discussions and behaviors. Organizational style is explicitly different from the leadership or management styles of individual members of the organization.
- **Staff** is the management of people as a pool of embodied resources. In high-performing organizations, the staff must be nurtured with a positive work environment, opportunities to do good work, and rewards for doing so. Staff must also be supported in their training and development to maintain critical knowledge and skills. Guarding the members of an organization against physical and psychological

[5] Philip Selznick, *Leadership in Administration: A Sociological Interpretation*, University of California Press, 1957.

stressors is another necessity for managing staff performance. Finally, staff must be allocated correctly and effectively to tasks.

- **Structure** divides tasks across an organization, decentralizing them for more-efficient management and alignment to areas with specific knowledge, processes, and tools. An organization's structure also provides coordination among its functions to allow communication and support integration and recentralization. Primary influences on structure include organizational size, complexity, flexibility, and risk aversion.
- **Strategy** consists of an organization's responses in reaction to anticipated and actual changes in its external environment. An organization's strategy is its way of communicating how it creates value for stakeholders. Henry Mintzberg concluded that the correct formulation of strategy should reflect a hybrid of analysis and intuition; he examined what he termed the *grand fallacy* of strategic planning: that such planning is not formulation. He offered that pure intuition is usually insufficient, given the complexity of the strategic environment, but that pure analysis reinforces existing structures and offers little chance for creative restructuring or innovation.[6] This consideration of strategy allows an organization to adapt to changes that challenge assumptions.
- **Systems** are the processes, procedures, tools, and other means by which an organization transforms inputs into outputs. As such, a system can be part of a single department or cover an entire organization, as needed. Systems in high-performance organizations are often well documented, sometimes to demonstrate compliance with international, governmental, industrial, educational, or other standards. Well-designed systems are also often integrated with each other so that outputs from one serve as inputs to another. This integration serves to enhance organizational effectiveness through intra- and interdepartmental cohesion and collective purpose.

The final detail needed to understand the framework is the division of the seven interdependent factors into groups that the original 7-S authors labeled *hard* and *soft*. The factors of strategy, structure, and systems were branded as hard because they deal with the perception of neutrality, precision, and facts. The soft factors, shared values, skills, style, and staff, relate to the perception of subjectivity, generalities, and beliefs. A final critical note on the division of hard and soft factors comes from Tom Peters, one of the codevelopers of the model:

> "Hard is soft. Soft is hard." That is, it's the plans and the numbers that are often "soft" (e.g., the sky-high soundness scores that the ratings agencies gave packages of dubious mortgages). And the people ("staff") and shared values ("corporate culture") and skills ("core competencies" these days) which are truly "hard"—that is, the bedrock upon which the adaptive and enduring enterprise is built.[7]

The question remains, then: How should OHSS approach the tasks critical to its establishment as an organization using the McKinsey 7-S framework?

In the establishment of any new organization, activities must be enacted and deliverables produced for each of the seven factors of the McKinsey 7-S framework. The context of the organization, its purpose, its people, and an innumerable list of other things ultimately determine what activities and what deliverables are required. DHS established OHSS to maximize data transparency and consistency, support data-driven decisionmaking, and improve the efficiency of statistical reporting. In the rest of this chapter, we expand on each of the 7-S factors, deriving the contents of our discussion from the organizational development literature,

---

[6] Henry Mintzberg, *The Rise and Fall of Strategic Planning: Reconceiving Roles for Planning, Plans, Planners*, Free Press, 1994.

[7] Tom Peters, "A Brief History of the 7-S ('McKinsey 7-S') Model," blog post, January 9, 2011.

historical examples, and interviews with representatives of various FSAs. These data have been collected, collated, and categorized according to the 7-S factors to establish objectives and supporting tasks that will result in an OHSS that complies with all statutory and regulatory requirements while exhibiting the structure, culture, and workforce needed to meet the high expectations of its internal and external stakeholders.

## Crafting a Target Operating Model for the Office of Homeland Security Statistics

Building on the various research methods for this study, including literature review, interviews with current and former FSA leadership, and the development of the LM as validated through the DHS workshop, we can define the target operating model for OHSS for implementation. In the rest of this section, we discuss each of the 7-S factors in turn.

### Shared Values

Shared values are an intangible but critical component of an organization's culture: They play a major role in guiding decisions and determining behaviors. Although an organization's desired values are established by its founders, a mature organization's values are influenced by the personally held values of every member of that organization. Healthy organizations possess three areas of alignment of their shared values:

- The **stated organizational values** are aligned with the **perceived organizational values**.
- **Individuals' values and beliefs** are aligned with those of the organization, at least broadly.
- The **organizational values** are aligned with the **purpose and goals of the organization**.

Reviews of relevant academic and government literature and interviews with SMEs revealed three overarching value sets that answer the questions "Who is OHSS?" "What does OHSS do?" and "How does OHSS operate?"

The first value set determines and expresses **who OHSS is**: The office must establish and maintain its identity as ***the* PSA** for DHS. Beyond the legal and statutory grounds for doing so, a shared understanding of this simple purpose will guide decisionmaking at all levels of the organization to enhance member engagement and loyalty.

Moreover, interviewees from other FSAs stressed that autonomy was essential to OHSS fulfilling this role. To ensure the integrity of its analysis, reports, and other outputs, the office's activities must be free from even the perception of political interference. As the establisher of statistical standards for DHS and a producer of federal reports used to inform law and policy, OHSS must maintain both actual independence and stakeholders' perception thereof. Members of OHSS must exhibit behaviors that demonstrate a lack of undue influence from others through organizational and personal relationships. Experts have noted that problems in FSA objectivity and credibility typically emerge from having too little autonomy, not too much. They recommend strong and clear language in statutes and internal guidelines to bolster that value.[8]

The second value set indicates **what OHSS does** and consists of three values aligned to the technical business of OHSS: **high-quality** data and analysis, **high-value** data and analysis, **secure** data, and **secure** func-

[8] Constance F. Citro, Jonathan Auerbach, Katherine Smith Evans, Erica L. Groshen, J. Steven Landefeld, Jeri Mulrow, Thomas Petska, Steve Pierson, Nancy Potok, Charles J. Rothwell, John Thompson, James L. Woodworth, and Edward Wu, "What Protects the Autonomy of the Federal Statistical Agencies? An Assessment of the Procedures in Place to Protect the Independence and Objectivity of Official U.S. Statistics," *Statistics and Public Policy*, Vol. 10, No. 1, 2023.

tions. The value of high quality guides members of OHSS to exhibit behaviors of appropriate data sourcing, analytical rigor, identification and mitigation of biases, QA and QC, and so on. The worth of high value ensures that members of OHSS always act with the stakeholder in mind and therefore deliver products and services that are timely, credible, and relevant to known or anticipated stakeholder needs. Because DHS is a government agency accountable for the data and information of millions of Americans and others, the value of security is indisputable. Security as a value goes beyond rote compliance with systemic and structural requirements, to an intrinsic concern in its members for the protection of all OHSS processes, procedures, and data.

### 7-S Workshop Discussion Theme: OHSS Shared Values

Many of the themes elicited throughout the LM sessions surfaced during the 7-S discussion that focused on shared values. Participants acknowledged that ethical practices should serve as the "core of who OHSS is." Furthermore, they acknowledged that OHSS should be known for serving as a trusted provider for authenticating and validating data, abiding by all applicable federal and departmental laws and compliance policies to ensure data collection and analysis integrity (i.e., serving as effective data "stewards"), maintaining rules for how data are protected, and ensuring robust whistleblower protections ("stronger than the rest of the department") to maintain agency independence.

The third and final value set consists of four values that describe **how OHSS operates**: the structure and operation of OHSS, resulting in an organization that is lean, efficient, and transparent. Lean organizations are often hierarchically flat and use the minimum amount of resources required to accomplish tasks. As a value, organizational leanness results in members with more skill and flexibility who are empowered to make decisions and changes that improve the organization. Because OHSS is a new organization, its structure and systems are expected to need frequent adjustment; having a value of leanness safeguards the organization against changes that add unnecessary layers or steps. **Efficiency** in operations is a similar value to the lean organization, with a greater focus on day-to-day systems and skills. The organizational value of efficiency leads to behaviors that eliminate inefficiencies revealed by regular reviews of OHSS's process maps, skill inventories, and other organizational documentation. Organizational **transparency** as a value guides OHSS members to act in ways that provide clarity to stakeholders and increase their trust in the organization's independence while guaranteeing the accountability critical to the public sector. Transparency can also paradoxically augment the statistical authority value; admitting a lack of knowledge in one area can increase stakeholder confidence in other data.

The shared set of values developed for and with OHSS serves as a starting point. These values are somewhat aspirational as a core component of OHSS's desired organizational structure. They are not, however, something to set and forget at the outset of planning the organization. Every member of the organization, through their behaviors, gets to vote every day on what the true values of OHSS are. If the combined weight of the members' enacted values is not aligned with the stated or desired values, the organization will undergo an unplanned change that will affect the other factors of the 7-S framework. The following list summarizes the design principles for OHSS shared values, according to our analysis of shared-value statements made by interviewees and further refined during the in-person workshop:

- Who is OHSS?
  - OHSS is a PSA.
- What does OHSS do?
  - Provide high-quality data and analysis.
  - Provide high-value data and analysis.

  - Provide secure data.
  - Provide secure functions.
- How does OHSS operate?
  - with low overhead
  - efficiently
  - transparently
  - independently.

### Policy Implication

- Promulgate a principle memorandum to communicate OHSS's nature and (dual) role.

## Skills

The skills needed in an organization's members reflect the purpose and goals of that organization. Changes to the organization will result in changes to the individual and collective skills needed by the organization. Therefore, management must continuously evaluate the individual and collective skills within its purview. Healthy organizations have a keen awareness of

- the set of skills critical to organizational success
- each member's skill performance compared to established standards
- maintained skills that are no longer required after organizational changes
- skill gaps or underskilling requiring training or development.

The skills and knowledge needed by the members of a nascent OHSS must be aligned to the stated purpose of the organization's founding, as well as with all other factors identified in the 7-S framework. The training requirements identified for OHSS through the data elicitation and feedback processes include training on the purpose of statistical standards and the role of OHSS in their management; on key skills and knowledge for OHSS employees; on the OHSS QA and QC programs; on data-sharing and reporting; and on data security. In each of these areas, OHSS must define its training needs. Organizational training needs can be identified by evaluating and connecting the skills held by its staff, required by its systems, advantageous to its style, and aligned to its strategy. Once it has identified these training needs, OHSS must create or otherwise procure appropriate training and make it available to the appropriate and, in most cases, internal stakeholders. However, some training might also be needed by DHS or broader stakeholder groups. In keeping training and development recommended practices, those who receive training must have opportunities for its implementation in real-world situations and for providing feedback on the value of the training. Throughout the entire process, the existence of and requirement for training must be communicated to the appropriate stakeholders. Subsequent reevaluation of skills should take place on a regular or ongoing basis, as determined by the organization.

Interviewees noted two issues related to skills:

- First, several FSAs rely on seconded or part-time staff for many of their analytic functions. Those people are, however, sometimes not eligible for on-the-job training that is available to full-time employees. In addition, the hiring schedule and throughput can affect training opportunities. Training is worthwhile only if there are enough trainees and DHS can expect them to stay in their positions long enough to make that investment worthwhile.
- Second, interviewees mentioned that rotations between OHSS and DHS components could improve understanding of processes, definitions, and methodologies of both entities. Rotated staff members

already serve as critical bridges between OHSS and its internal stakeholders, facilitating data-sharing and familiarizing their home components with OHSS's mission and purpose.

### 7-S Workshop Discussion Theme: OHSS Skills

Discussions about skills within the 7-S model generally focused on ensuring that OHSS will have diverse staff with a wide variety of skill sets to support daily operational activities. Participants suggested that OHSS would require extensive training on OHSS mission, operations, and context within the larger FSA and stakeholder ecosystem. Participants indicated that OHSS should consider instituting an onboarding program for new hires to instill a baseline understanding of component efforts and applicable (both existing and potential) data streams and protection measures. Some participants noted that training materials would also need to focus on budgeting, human-resource functions, and website functionality for OHSS staff billeted for support positions. Others highlighted that selecting staff with existing expertise (e.g., "statisticians who work with immigration data are immigration experts") to provide additional meaning to the data analyzed. Finally, some participants suggested that establishing (and institutionalizing) peer-to-peer training and exchange programs with other FSAs could help OHSS maintain situational awareness on statistical community best practices.

The following list summarizes the design principles for desired OHSS staff skills and knowledge areas, according to our analysis of statements made by interviewees on the skills necessary to the success of OHSS, which were further refined during the in-person workshop:

- Understand the purpose of statistical standards.
- Understand OHSS's role in managing statistical standards.
- Know how to use the DHS statistical standards database (DSSD), once implemented.
- Display other key individual skills and knowledge identified as necessary for OHSS employees.
- Enact OHSS QA and QC programs.
- Enact OHSS processes for data-sharing and reporting.
- Enact OHSS data security tools and activities.

### Policy Implication

- Develop directives on rotational assignments and detailee requirements to enable component statistical staff to better understand OHSS mission and operations.

## Style

An organization's style is a result of its collective leadership and management styles. Another intangible component of organizations, style is often revealed through observation of the business functions, subordinate teams, stakeholder relationships, and other items on which the organization's leaders and managers spend their time and attention. Healthy organizations often exhibit markers of organizational style, such as

- members participating in decisionmaking
- engagement with improvement initiatives at multiple levels of the organization
- appetite for professional, but not interpersonal, conflict
- healthy intergroup competition and cooperation across functions.

OHSS's foundational culture will be determined by its initial set of leaders. These leaders can get a head start on establishing an intentionally positive and high-performing culture by leveraging the data collec-

### 7-S Workshop Discussion Theme: OHSS Style

Three key observations arose from the workshop module focused on OHSS style:

- First, participants noted that, as OHSS "dramatically" increases in size in the next several years, planning will need to accommodate potential changes in organizational scope and mission.
- Second, as OHSS continues to grow (as will the number of external RFIs), staff will need to ensure a balance between data quality, data analysis, and deliverable timeliness, ensuring that data quality, analytical rigor, ethical practices, and transparency about office limitations feature prominently throughout the organization.
- Third, as the group discussed, at length, components will need to validate OHSS reporting while maintaining independence and promoting collaboration between and among components. One existing gap that could affect OHSS products in the near future is a lack of internal guidance about how to relay or inform data origins without informing component methodologies.

tion and analysis from this study. Input elicited from SMEs and members of similar organizations indicates that a culture ideal for OHSS's stated purpose exhibits an organizational style characterized by two major trends:

- a technically proficient culture of statistical accuracy, authority, authenticity, and security
- an inclusive, team-of-teams approach to statistical analysis and reporting.

Active communication of OHSS's organizational style is crucial during the first few years of the organization's existence and will remain extremely important after it is fully established. The use of multiple and varied communication channels, such as spoken, printed, and demonstrative, increases the likelihood that organization members will receive information in a form that they will find useful and applicable. Interviewees said that OHSS leadership and management must support the office's role as the department's standardization authority, emphasizing the benefits of standardization to large, distributed organizations, especially in the public sector. OHSS will also be served by the creation of a culture of statistical accuracy and authority. The production of accurate and useful analyses and reports is central to OHSS's purpose, one that would be damaged by a lack of appropriate rigor in sourcing data and conducting analysis. Establishing an organizational identity of statistical authority within DHS would create a common understanding that OHSS has power derived from its specialized knowledge and can, accordingly, inform relevant decisions and actions for DHS and the broader government. OHSS's culture must also highlight the importance of data security and authenticity to each of its members. Finally, OHSS's culture must recognize the knowledge and experience of its own members and of subordinate statistical offices and stakeholders. It should integrate existing statistical offices and functions into a shared culture while maintaining appropriate autonomy and identity. As a new organization, OHSS should leverage the previous structures, cultures, systems, and relationships of its predecessors, peers, and stakeholders as appropriate, centralizing only essential functions to emphasize a team-of-teams organizational style.

A proactive stance on leadership style can also help support OHSS's institutional and analytical autonomy. Department principals can desire having input to or receiving early disclosure of an FSA's findings and reports. This can be driven by concerns about blowback over bad news, for example. However, statutes could clearly establish the FSA director as terminally responsible for all the agency's outputs. This would provide political cover for principals while further isolating the FSA's activities. The following list summarizes the design principles for OHSS style, according to our analysis of interviewees' statements (stakeholders reviewed and refined the draft principles during the in-person workshop; what follows are the OHSS-adopted principles):

- Support the office's role as DHS's standardization authority.
- Create a culture of statistical accuracy and authority.
- Integrate DHS's statistical offices into a shared culture while maintaining those offices' appropriate autonomy and identities.
- Centralize only essential functions to emphasize team-of-teams leadership.
- Highlight the importance of data security and authenticity to every role in the organization.
- Communicate regularly with internal and external stakeholders through multichannel messages.

### Policy Implications

- Develop a directive outlining the scope and role of component review of OHSS products.
- Develop guidance on approaches to relaying and informing data origins rather than informing component methods.

## Staff

An organization's staff is ultimately how it accomplishes its mission. Therefore, this drives a need for people with specific KSAs and whose values are aligned to those of the organization. Some tools, such as job analyses, can help determine the human requirements of jobs and the context in which those jobs occur.[9] In a healthy organization, the management and leadership teams are heavily involved in

- staff selection
- role allocation
- member engagement
- reward systems
- staff development
- protection of staff.

As OHSS is established, it must create its foundational staffing needs. One first step would be to conduct a job analysis and develop competency assessment frameworks. In a postpandemic context, modernized organizations have incorporated additional considerations for members, including the mobility, technoliteracy, community, and creativity needs of its workforce.[10] These considerations provide additional opportunities for engagement by members of the organization because they allow an increase in the integration of each member's professional and personal, public, and private identities. Such integration has been shown to improve workplace performance by several quantitative and qualitative measures.

To the degree possible, OHSS should establish ways of thinking and communicating that focus on roles rather than positions. Although a position is defined by its title and location in the organization, the roles that individuals play are dynamic and adaptable, with a focus on how they add value to the organization. Another way of developing OHSS's members and simultaneously reinforcing the organization's values and strategy would be to cultivate exchange opportunities between OHSS and other statistical offices to enhance collaboration and technical and cultural understanding. Finally, the importance of data security identified across

---

9 U.S. Office of Personnel Management, "Job Analysis," webpage, undated.

10 Zincir and Tunç, 2017.

### 7-S Workshop Discussion Theme: OHSS Staff

Many of the themes elicited in the skill session were reiterated in the staff section of the exercise (e.g., diverse staff with applicable skill sets), although participants offered a more granular view of the types of skills required for mission success. For example, participants discussed the need for some staff to serve as generalists with a broad technical knowledge base; for other specialists with domain-specific expertise, including data-processing specialists (e.g., SAS and Python SMEs), data-curation specialists, and disclosure-review specialists; and for other staff with talent-management expertise to ensure OHSS workforce continuity. Participants also noted that OHSS should consider incentives and highlight career-pathway programs (e.g., awards, recognition), given DHS's historical difficulties in hiring and retaining staff for statistical functions across the enterprise. Some participants suggested that cross-training staff in various functions could help address short-term workforce shortages. Motivation (which is, according to the group discussions, closely associated with retention) proved to be another especially important topic among participants. Discussants noted that OHSS should seek to create a culture that encourages staff cohesion and ensure that there are processes and procedures in place to protect staff from "unreasonable requests" and from being "excoriated by members of Congress and the public" because of potentially unpopular policy changes influenced by their analysis. Discussants offered providing situational awareness to OHSS staff (e.g., ensuring that staff are provided with context about stakeholder requests and why it is "important") as one potential mitigation measure.

multiple 7-S framework factors compels the formation of one or more associated roles within OHSS. Consequently, OHSS should sponsor a statistical data security group to discuss, inform, and make data security recommendations.

The FSA interviewees provided several recommendations on the selection process for the OHSS director. Most indicated a preference for having the director be a presidentially appointed position requiring Senate approval. Qualifications should be spelled out in statute, they said, and the director's term should not coincide with a presidential term. Senate approval is key, they noted, enhancing the director's status and independent authority and providing a non–executive branch oversight channel for OHSS. Interviewees noted that, if the Senate is not going to approve a nominee, promoting the OHSS director from among career personnel would be better than having a presidential appointee.

Last, the interviewees recommended that OHSS have full hiring authority for its personnel—ideally, written in a department-wide regulation. In other FSAs, hiring decisions belong to the department or to offices at higher echelons. Those entities have sometimes determined not only the number of billets but also the positions for which the FSA could hire. This has introduced misalignment between FSA needs and resources and, potentially, the longer-term effect of undermining the agency's autonomy. The following list summarizes the design principles for OHSS staff, according to our analysis of statements about staff needs made by interviewees and further refined during the in-person workshop:

- Conduct an OHSS job analysis to inform the design of a proficient and professional workforce.
- Consider the mobility, technoliteracy, community, and creativity needs of the workforce.
- Shift organizational thinking to fulfilling roles rather than positions.
- Support exchange opportunities between OHSS and SOs for enhanced technical and cultural understanding.
- Sponsor a statistical data security group to discuss, inform, and make data security recommendations.

## Policy Implication

- Develop policy to establish a statistical data security group organized to discuss, inform, and make data security recommendations.

## Structure

Organizational structure, such as that laid out in organizational charts and other diagrams, is often the most visible of the 7-S factors. At its core, however, an organization's structure serves only two functions: to divide labor and to coordinate across the organization's components. Considerations that inform an organization's structure include the organization's size, complexity, type of work, flexibility, and attitude toward risk. Healthy organizations balance their structure against

- degree of centralization of control and decisionmaking
- coordination and communication required to maintain cohesiveness
- physical or temporal proximity to the necessary workforce, infrastructure, and materials.

The best structure for OHSS should be determined by answering questions about how the organization and its subordinate structures are defined from a task and role perspective and about what OHSS's relationship should be with DHS and other FSAs. Feedback from data collected from the FSA community indicated that, when determining OHSS's position in the DHS hierarchy, a balance must be struck between (1) increased influence and attention if at a higher level of DHS and (2) increased independence and protection from influence if located in lower layers of the department.

In general, the interviewees recommended that OHSS be located at as high an echelon as possible—ideally, directly under the Secretary of Homeland Security. The interviewees noted that, although embedding OHSS within a lower-echelon entity could offer some protection from influence, FSAs must be apolitical but politically savvy. Navigating shifting politics is an essential activity for OHSS, regardless of where it is placed. But situating the office under another entity adds layers between OHSS and principal decisionmakers, potentially increasing the difficulty of having the office's needs and requests heard, decided on, and addressed. Furthermore, the FSA interviewees noted the importance of budgetary and personnel authority. In addition to the hiring challenges described above, control over budgets and disbursement would prevent the office's budget from being cannibalized or diverted by higher-echelon entities.

Whatever the final position of OHSS, the drawbacks of the

### 7-S Workshop Discussion Themes: OHSS Structure

Discussions about existing OHSS structure focused primarily on the challenges and enablers of functional versus topical (or domain-based) organizations. Many participants noted that, although OHSS likely represents a functional organization (as of November 2023), OHSS might assume various topical-based characteristics as it becomes matrixed among DHS components (e.g., immigration, maritime focus). Some members expressed that OHSS should remain a purely functional office to ensure objectivity within data governance processes and activities. Others suggested that a hybrid model (functional and topical) might allow OHSS to be more flexible and responsive as it matures. The discussion of a hybrid approach led to additional exchanges about the conflict between serving as a public source for authoritative data and lending data and analyses to support internal decisionmaking. The group concluded that the OHSS structure might eventually need to consider changing to fulfill both functions. Finally, participants emphasized that, regardless of organizational construct sought, a structure for communicating data governance had not been established and would be required to maintain unity of effort.

choice must be considered and addressed through the factors of shared values, style, systems, and other means. For OHSS, mapping techniques that are likely to make the most sense include stakeholder maps, responsibility assignment matrices (closely related to the system function of the 7-S framework), and information flow diagrams. As previously discussed in the "Style" section, OHSS's independence and authority are critical to its purpose. Therefore, its structure should reflect a decentralized approach to its subordinate structures so that they retain maximum autonomy and identity, centralizing only the data and essential functions necessary for OHSS to operate effectively. Part of the recommended structure for OHSS is the creation of an OHSS AC, for which a charter must be drafted with feedback and buy-in from its anticipated members. The purpose of an OHSS AC would be to enable component stakeholders to have a voice in codesigning the relationships between their offices and OHSS, within guidelines, by helping develop the scaffolding structures that will define these relationships. The approved version of the charter and any related documents that are created in support of the OHSS AC must be maintained and updated as required. As part of OHSS's overall communication plan, the AC's purpose and activities must be communicated to its stakeholders through relevant channels and at appropriate intervals. The following list summarizes the design principles for OHSS structure, according to our analysis of statements about OHSS's organizational structure made by interviewees and further refined during the in-person workshop:

- Develop division of labor according to areas of knowledge, processes, and tools.
- Establish centralized, rather than decentralized, control for increased unity of effort for better communication within partitions.
- Create mapping according to the location of physical assets, how information flows, how materials flow, where decisions are made and by whom, and so on.
- Establish an OHSS AC.

### Policy Implications

- Establish a structure for communicating data governance approaches and related requirements for component data governance.
- Develop guidance to define a functional, topical, or (more likely) hybrid structure for OHSS.
- Develop directives on OHSS's role in enabling component data analysis and reporting.

## Strategy

An organization's strategy documents its plans for reacting to external changes in the market or other context. A strong strategy is built on data and analysis for long-term sustainability but also provides leaders and managers the flexibility to make quick decisions in response to events as they occur. In a healthy organization, the strategy clearly describes

- expectations of organizational performance
- a common direction around which members can rally
- anticipated responses to changes in stakeholder demands
- a professional approach to achieving the organization's purpose.

The strategy that OHSS uses must be derived from the office's purpose and place within the larger mission of DHS. The OHSS strategy can be developed through the common planning process of validating its vision and mission; setting SMART goals in short, medium, and long time horizons; establishing metrics; publishing; and communicating the strategy to stakeholders. As a new organization, OHSS should emphasize its long-term goals, perhaps five to seven years in the future. Although, because of internal and external organizational changes, long-term goals are less likely to be met as written, they communicate a common direction to members and stakeholders that can show the way when day-to-day issues and challenges threaten to push the team off course. We recommend regular reviews of the strategy, especially in the first few years, as OHSS gains first-hand experience in its execution, but major revisions could lead to confusion and misalignment that result in poor organizational performance. If OHSS's management and members believe in the organization's strategy, the tactics and maneuvers that make up its execution will be able to take advantage of the opportunities that present themselves. OHSS has already expressed a strength it can leverage through a desire for its work to be described as *credible*, *accurate*, *relevant*, *timely*, and *authoritative*. These words provide ready-made touchstones that can serve as the core of OHSS's goals and objectives. One additional descriptor also previously desired by OHSS is the *objectivity* of its data and reports. Contemporary data science recognizes the functional impossibility of truly objective data being collected and analyzed by humans or human-designed machines.[11] Instead, OHSS should use the descriptor *comprehensive* to reflect the importance of collecting and analyzing data from multiple sources and perspectives, using multiple methods to synthesize findings that reflect a more comprehensive understanding of the topic. Relevant to the cultural style of the organization is that OHSS must ensure that the resulting organizational strategy includes SOs as stakeholders. In some cases, interviewees said, SOs have been conducting similar activities in much the same organizational context that OHSS will have, so the knowledge they have gained and lessons they have learned must be recognized and respected. Two topics identified in the structured interviews and literature review as being crucial to the strategy of a nascent OHSS are data security and stakeholder management. Although these and similar topics are often treated only in the systems and sometimes the structure of an organization, their inclusion in the strategy confirms their importance to the organization and builds them into its foundation. The following list summarizes the design principles for OHSS strategy, according to our analysis of strategy statements made by interviewees and further refined during the in-person workshop:

- Produce credible reports by consistently referencing validated data and using established analytical techniques.
- Ensure the accuracy of DHS statistical data and reports through annual audits of the OHSS QA and QC programs.

### 7-S Workshop Discussion Themes: The OHSS Strategy

Participants in the 7-S strategy session emphasized OHSS's role in

- championing data literacy across DHS (ensuring a comprehensive understanding of statistical data's role in decision-making, with the CDO acting for data value and the SO serving as advocate for data literacy)
- maintaining an explicit strategic position that showcases compliance with relevant regulations, statutes, and policies that govern statistical agency behavior
- ensuring distinction between statistical and operational stakeholder requests (i.e., that components focus on curating operational data and OHSS focus solely on statistical RFIs)
- establishing clear lanes and SOPs for addressing external FOIA requests (i.e., OHSS would turn FOIA requests over to components and allow them to delegate, although OHSS would remain available to respond to specific questions and validate component responses)
- establishing authority to fulfill or deny external RFIs (e.g., OHSS might not have relevant authority for either until FSA status is formalized).

[11] Melanie Feinberg, "The Myth of Objective Data," *MIT Press Reader*, April 17, 2023.

- Apply knowledge gained through stakeholder communication to enhance the relevance of OHSS activities.
- Respond to external RFIs in a timely manner by providing at least a minimal viable response within the provided window, coordinating for additional time as required to meet quality and other standards.
- Provide regular development opportunities for the DHS statistics community to establish and maintain OHSS's authority.
- Identify and acknowledge bias through the triangulation of data, analysts, theories, and methodologies to produce reports with a more comprehensive picture of the subject.

### Policy Implications

- Draft and circulate SOPs to address OHSS's role in supporting responses to FOIA requests.
- Draft and circulate SOPs to address OHSS's role in fulfilling external RFIs (statistical stakeholder requests).
- Develop guidance and education aids to advance statistical data literacy across DHS to help ensure a comprehensive understanding of statistical data's role in decisionmaking systems.

## Systems

An organization's systems are the processes, procedures, and tools that its members use to fulfill its purpose. A system might be used by only one member of an organization, or it might be employed organization-wide, depending on its purpose. Organizational systems are commonly documented in formats that reflect the formality and style of their primary user groups but might affect other groups or individuals as well. In a healthy organization, systems

- are sufficiently documented in accessible formats
- use diagrams or other methods to identify process shortfalls
- ensure interoperability and clear communication when systems cross functional lines
- are fit for use and do not levy undue burden on the members who use them.

The systems that OHSS needs are linked to its fundamental purposes, established by its strategy and structure, while also being mutually supportive of the other 7-S framework factors.[12] SMEs we interviewed identified and recommended more systems than they identified or recommended any of the other 7-S factors. OHSS's systems must be established while taking into account its desired status as an RSAU, maintaining its independence in all functions. These recommendations can be categorized into five groups of systems, which we list here with no intent to communicate an order of priority. The first system recommendation for OHSS implementation is the creation of a DSSD to serve as the single, unifying registry of statistical standards for DHS.

To establish the DSSD, OHSS must develop the requirements for the database and conduct an alternatives analysis to assess the effectiveness, costs, and risks of alternative ways of meeting those requirements. Once a solid set of requirements has been developed, OHSS should draft a request for proposals outlining its desired DSSD system, procure the selected solution, and transition that procured solution to operations for use and maintenance in accordance with departmental requirements and acquisition policies.

The second set of system recommendations focuses on the need for OHSS to establish the organizational policies, guidance processes, procedures, and tools that it needs as DHS's authority on statistical standards

[12] Zincir and Tunç, 2017.

management and the handling of statistical data. This broad group of systems will support OHSS in achieving its strategic goals for the production and dissemination of comprehensive, credible, accurate, relevant, timely, and authoritative statistical information and analysis. We have already identified one specific policy as crucial to maintaining OHSS's neutrality: that OHSS tasks and deliverables will not directly support enforcement activities within DHS. For this second set of systems, OHSS should enact a process of creating the relevant documentation, obtaining feedback and support from appropriate stakeholders, publishing the documentation where it will be readily accessible to the appropriate stakeholders, and communicating the resulting systems to stakeholders through relevant channels.

A third set of recommendations for OHSS's systems focuses on the need for processes and procedures related to the production and dissemination of statistical reports by DHS and its components' statistical organizations. These systems should also cover the release of statistical information and analysis to external agencies in response to RFIs. The interviewees stressed that OHSS must establish and adhere to a strict timetable for the release of its statistical products. Such a regularized timetable serves as a commitment mechanism and increases OHSS's autonomy and credibility. Consistently hitting reporting steps assures outside audiences of the office's competence and provides fewer opportunities for political influence.

The fourth set of OHSS systems relates to the office's establishment or adoption of data security policies, processes, and procedures. The secure storage and handling of statistical data are directly correlated to stakeholder trust in OHSS and the successful achievement of its duties. Strong data protection systems are particularly important for OHSS. It is simultaneously tasked with conducting statistical analysis and supporting DHS decisions. To comply with OMB and other guidelines, the office must ensure that its analysis cannot be used to identify specific people, a task often needed for law enforcement functions. Consequently, the FSA interviewees universally noted the importance of strong firewalls between OHSS's statistical and administra-

### 7-S Workshop Discussion Themes: OHSS Systems

The final 7-S module elicited some discussions about existing IT and data infrastructures and served as an opportunity for OHSS and component representatives to follow up on many of the previous points made throughout the course of the workshop. The OHSS representatives noted that there was no data-reporting environment beyond the DSSD and that OHSS continued to undergo IT modernization. Part of this modernization effort will include transferring authoritative data into a database rather than SAS files, which OHSS staff would clean and validate. Modernization of data-reporting systems will also be required to meet various data standards stipulated in DHS reporting requirements (e.g., DHS Policy Directive 4300A).[a] OHSS's IT modernization efforts are reportedly facing some timeliness issues because various contractors have performed different upgrades to existing systems (and are further "beholden to OCIO limitations and requirements"). Other topics discussed in this section centered on

- accessing restricted (classified) data (i.e., although OHSS does not maintain classified data, staff might "infrequently access classified intel products to inform projections" for items related to terrorism and targeted violence)
- ensuring that components understand what provided data will be used for
- maintaining a shared methodology to facilitate data assimilation (i.e., making sure the "numbers match")
- standardizing access points, traceability, and maintenance of data ingested by OHSS systems (while keeping component data systems as the systems of record for raw data).

[a] DHS, *DHS Sensitive Systems*, Policy Directive 4300A, version 13.1, July 17, 2017.

tive support functions. In particular, they highlighted that OHSS must coordinate closely between the office's IT services and those of the department. OMB guidelines impose additional restrictions on data access and manipulation beyond normal IT standards.

A fifth set of recommendations for OHSS systems is the establishment of QA and QC programs. Once the organization's needs have been determined and extant internal and external models for quality management reviewed, OHSS should create, publish, and communicate information about the program to its stakeholders. Additionally, part of the QA and QC program must also be an internal audit process for regularly evaluating the quality of the organization's work and products. Many of these systems, as well as additionally identified systems, are suitable for documentation within a DHS statistical data management instruction maintained by OHSS for the department. Finally, OHSS must develop processes and procedures related to its RSAU mission. The development, documentation, and implementation of systems pertinent to the organization's purpose and integrated with its shared values and strategic vision will ensure that OHSS's daily activities are maintained by its skills, style, staff, and structural factors.[13]

The sixth and final set of system recommendations would establish structured communication and coordination with DHS stakeholders. Unlike most other FSAs, OHSS will ingest data primarily from department components, rather than conducting its own surveys. Good relationships with DHS stakeholders are therefore essential to gaining access to, standardizing, and conducting analysis on department data. Thus far, the DHS interviewees have expressed appreciation for OHSS's efforts on the SO Council. They said that that body was a constructive forum in which to raise and resolve issues and to familiarize themselves with OHSS's mission and plans. Further discussion of OHSS stakeholder engagement can be found in Chapter 5. Table 6.1 summarizes this section of the report based on our analysis of statements made by interviewees on the systems needed for OHSS to be successful. The initial list was reviewed and refined during the in-person workshop.

[13] Robert H. Waterman, Jr., Thomas J. Peters, and Julien R. Phillips, "Structure Is Not Organization," *Business Horizons*, Vol. 23, No. 3, June 1980.

TABLE 6.1
## Design Principles for Establishing Office of Homeland Security Statistics Systems

| System | Steps Required to Establish Each System |
|---|---|
| Create a DSSD. | Develop the requirements for the DSSD. |
| | Analyze alternatives to assess the effectiveness, cost, and risks of alternative ways of meeting the requirements. |
| | Draft a request for proposals that outlines the desired DSSD system. |
| | Procure a DSSD solution. Establish departmental policy to integrate DSSD use across DHS. |
| | Transition the procured solution to operations for use and maintenance. |
| Establish standards management and statistical data policies, processes, and procedures. | Manage standards. |
| | Research the organization's needs and extant internal and external models for standards management. |
| | Write any necessary standards management policy. |
| | Create a DHS statistical standards instruction of processes and procedures. |
| | Publish the standards management documentation where it will be readily accessible to the appropriate stakeholders. |
| | Communicate the contents of the DHS statistical standards SOP to stakeholders through relevant channels, such as the SO Council. |
| | Develop and disseminate statistical data policies. |
| | Write a DHS statistical data sourcing policy. |
| | Write a DHS statistical accuracy and authority policy. |
| | Write OHSS guidance on identifying and acknowledging subjectivity in statistical analysis |
| | Create a DHS statistical data management instruction on processes and procedures. |
| | Publish the DHS statistical data management instruction where it will be readily accessible to the appropriate stakeholders. |
| | Communicate the contents of the DHS statistical data management SOP to stakeholders through relevant channels, such as the SO Council. |
| | Clarify OHSS scope as limited to data used for statistical purposes. |
| | Draft a policy stating that OHSS activities will not directly support enforcement within DHS. |
| | Obtain feedback and support of the policy from appropriate stakeholders. |
| | Publish the OHSS nonsupport-of-enforcement policy where it will be readily accessible to the appropriate stakeholders. |
| | Communicate the OHSS nonsupport-of-enforcement policy to stakeholders through relevant channels. |

## Table 6.1—Continued

| System | Steps Required to Establish Each System |
|---|---|
| Create reporting processes and procedures. | Research the organization's needs and extant internal and external models for reporting statistical data and analysis. |
| | Create a data request portion of the DHS statistical data management instruction. |
| | Create a data-sharing portion of the DHS statistical data management instruction. |
| Establish or adopt OHSS data security policies, processes, and procedures. | Perform data governance. |
| | Draft OHSS policies on the protection of data at rest and data in motion. |
| | Obtain feedback and support of the data security policies from appropriate stakeholders. |
| | Publish OHSS data security policies where they will be readily accessible to the appropriate stakeholders. |
| | Communicate OHSS data security policies to stakeholders through relevant channels. |
| | Manage data. |
| | Research the organization's needs and extant internal and external models for data security. |
| | Create a data security portion of the DHS statistical data management instruction. |
| Establish data QA and QC programs. | Research the organization's needs and extant internal and external models for quality management. |
| | Create the OHSS QA and QC program guide and any other necessary program documentation. |
| | Create an internal audit process for the OHSS QA and QC program. |
| | Publish all QA and QC program documentation where it will be readily accessible to the appropriate stakeholders. |
| | Communicate about the OHSS QA and QC program and documents to stakeholders through relevant channels. |
| Establish policies, processes, and procedures for stakeholder engagement. | Develop a communication plan. |
| | Draft the OHSS communication plan, aligned with DHS and other relevant extant communication plans. |
| | Obtain feedback and support of the plan from appropriate stakeholders. |
| | Publish the OHSS communication plan where it will be readily accessible to the appropriate stakeholders. |
| | Conduct regular reviews of the plan for updates and improvements needed to better meet stakeholders' needs. |
| | Develop and promulgate an engagement strategy. |
| | Create the OHSS engagement strategy using the personae developed for this project. |
| | Obtain feedback and support of the strategy from appropriate stakeholders. |
| | Publish the OHSS stakeholder engagement strategy where it will be readily accessible to the appropriate stakeholders. |
| | Conduct regular reviews of the strategy for updates and improvements needed to better meet stakeholders' needs. |

CHAPTER 7

# Recommendations

We conducted a substantial literature review and interviewed dozens of current and former SOs to develop input for a detailed LM and an organizational design framework.[1] We presented these draft models for validation at a workshop attended by OHSS staff and representatives from DHS component statistical activities in fall 2023. These insights informed a draft mission statement, supporting strategy pillars and objectives, a target operating model, and draft implementation guidance. The models in this report are those that OHSS adopted.

The creation of OHSS marks an important milestone in DHS's maturation by elevating statistical activities to a departmental function and seeking to enhance DHS decisionmaking through more-rigorous statistical analysis and public transparency. However, the office does not face an easy transition to its new role. The office must mature from one narrowly defined portfolio of DHS's mission—immigration—to cover all the data domains of the department. In the short term, OHSS will rely on other parts of DHS to provide it data, despite differing procedures for how those data are handled and stored. The office will need to balance its role as statistical office, in which it will support component needs and maintain productive relationships, with its goal of becoming an RSAU that maintains a level of independence that will be unique within DHS and likely, at least initially, not well understood by other parts of the department. OHSS will face tension with being transparent with Congress and the public while also safeguarding sensitive data.

Here we return to the study's research questions:

- What can be learned from existing analyses and open-source materials about the FSS?
  - Recent congressional and OMB guidance provides significant input to the challenge of establishing and measuring the effectiveness of a new RSAU.
- How can OHSS provide value to the components, in terms of both burden-sharing and advancing component statistical capacity and capabilities?
  - We developed a formal stakeholder engagement approach because OHSS's success relies heavily on collaboration with the component statistical activities.
- Who are the internal and external stakeholders that will engage with OHSS, and what are their goals, objectives, and likely challenges?
  - Part of the stakeholder engagement discussion included an approach for consolidating what is otherwise a dizzying list of potential stakeholders into a manageable list by framing each by characteristics of its relationship with OHSS.
- What tasks are associated with establishing an organization, and how should OHSS approach each of these establishing tasks?
  - We selected a leading organizational design framework to detail specific areas for implementation, including skills needed within OHSS staff and systems used to support OHSS functions. Insights from the fall 2023 workshop are integrated into our recommendations for the implementation plan;

[1] The organizational design framework was based largely on the McKinsey 7-S model described in Peters, 2011.

following up will communicate that the components are being heard and considered in the design of OHSS.

- What are the organizational inputs, outputs, outcomes, stakeholders, and activities that link OHSS activities to strategic objectives?
  - We developed an LM to address these elements of the OHSS organization—this served as a single-page communication to frame the fall 2023 workshop discussions. One future step could include using this LM to derive metrics—both those to measure outputs and those to measure mission outcomes.

## Recommendations: Crafting a Target Operating Model for Office of Homeland Security Statistics

To position the office to effectively accomplish its responsibilities, we developed several recommendations for organizational design and implementation, such as adopting the proposed mission statement, strategic pillars, and objectives and following up on implementation tasks aligned with the target operating model. Creating these involved the literature review and interviews with current and former SOs to understand best practices and lessons learned from existing FSAs. We then developed draft LMs and an organizational design framework based on the literature review and interviews. We validated these draft models through a workshop attended by OHSS staff and representatives from DHS component statistical activities in fall 2023. Using the insights from the literature review, interviews, and workshop, we developed the following recommendations, including mission statement, supporting strategy pillars and objectives, a target operating model, and draft implementation guidance:

- Develop and promulgate the following mission statement: "Foster transparency and data-driven homeland security decision-making by analyzing and disseminating timely, objective DHS data and statistics."[2]
- Adopt the following strategic pillars and objectives to communicate OHSS's approach to its mission and how to measure its success:
  - Maintain the official DHS statistical system of record.
  - Provide statistical data services to mature departmental statistical activities.
  - Produce independent reports as an RSAU.
- Follow up on implementation tasks and implied policy guidance aligned with the target operating model.
- Develop draft policy guidance to define authority and responsibilities regained by components.
- Develop policy guidance to address data standardization and analytic modeling and visualization for consistent data representation.

The strategic pillars and objectives and implementation plan included in this report reflect the aspects of organizational design and change identified in organizational theory literature. However, it is incumbent on

2 OHSS has already adopted this, and we include it in this report to represent a recommendation that could apply to future FSAs and to provide a full record of our analysis.

OHSS to position this strategy for successful execution in FYs 2024 and 2025. To execute its strategy, OHSS could choose to do any combination of the following:

- Identify short-term priorities that should be included in the next available budget request, and perform analysis to determine the amount of funding needed to execute those priorities.
- Determine medium- to long-term priorities that will require future resource requests, and plan for when those resources will be requested and the amount needed.
- Develop measures used to track progress with implementation of the strategy.

In the short term, OHSS must develop procedures to ensure the effective implementation of its separate missions related to its departmental statistical activities and its independent reporting activities. Such procedures could include ensuring that staff performing independent reporting activities maintain proper independence and communicate transparency about adherence to appropriate data standards. OHSS could examine the extent to which its budget should reflect these different missions and ensure that funding is separated to preserve the necessary independence. Commingling these missions without procedures in place to safeguard independence could have serious implications for OHSS's reputation within DHS, with the federal statistical community, and with the public.

Overall, this report answers the why, what, and how questions about standing up OHSS. Although this study and implementation guidance are specific to OHSS, we believe that the background information, research questions and methods, and areas of focus for implementation will be of use to the launch of any future FSA.

APPENDIX A

# The Office of Homeland Security Statistics Logic Model

This appendix supplements Chapter 4.

## An Overview of Logic Modeling

An LM is a graphical, at-a-glance view of an organization or a program and defines what the organization does and why—what it seeks to accomplish. It is a visual narrative explaining how the organization uses inputs in a series of major activities to create outputs, which, in turn, stakeholders employ to create positive outcomes. The same diagram also commonly shows the organization's overarching mission and major external factors that affect the organization's operations and performance. LMs also commonly show feedback (i.e., how the organization learns from its performance and realized outcomes to further improve). Figure A.1 is a sample template for an LM showing typical major elements and what they mean.

FIGURE A.1
**A Template for a Logic Model**

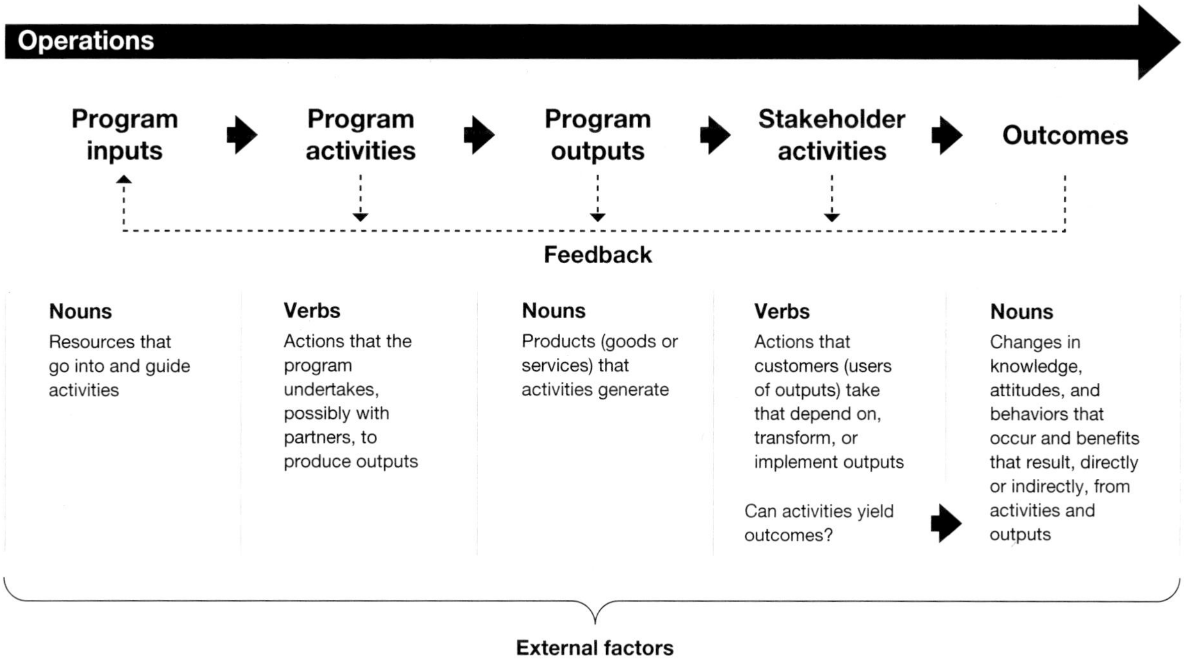


SOURCE: Adapted from Victoria A. Greenfield, Valerie L. Williams, and Elisa Eiseman, *Using Logic Models for Strategic Planning and Evaluation: Application to the National Center for Injury Prevention and Control*, RAND Corporation, TR-370-NCIPC, 2006, p. 4.

There is significant value in having a single, high-level map of what an organization does, how, and why. Example applications include the following:

- Validate organizational operations, whether current or planned (i.e., is there a reasonable narrative that explains how the activities and outputs will generate the desired outcomes?).
- Develop improved organizational plans in case deficiencies in said narrative are discovered after visualizing it.
- Explain the value proposition of the organization and its activities to internal and external stakeholders.
- Serve as a point of reference for planners and decisionmakers, helping them assess whether candidate ideas or investments are aligned with the organization's core purposes and activities, and helping answer whether the proposed actions would lead to improved outcomes.
- Serve as a point of reference for strategic planning and organizational performance management. Figure A.2 depicts a template showing how core strategic planning elements should align with key LM elements (e.g., overarching strategic goals and metrics should directly assess the outcomes, proximate goals and metrics should align with the day-to-day outputs the organization creates, and traditional management objectives and metrics on resource expenditures and work accomplished (e.g., tasks completed) should align with the organization's inputs and activities).

FIGURE A.2
**Aligning Strategic Planning Elements with Logic Model Elements**

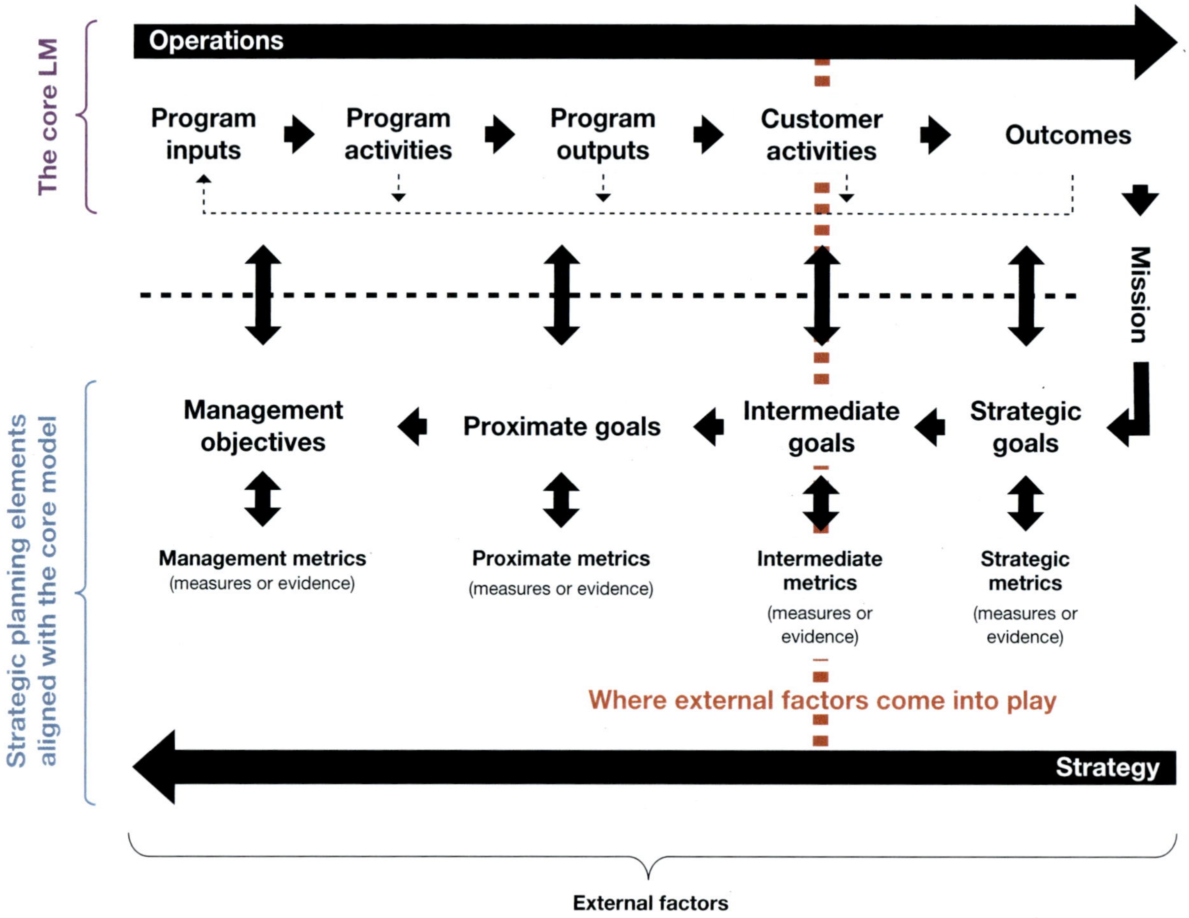


SOURCE: Adapted from Greenfield, Williams, and Eiseman, 2006, p. 4.

## Developing an Initial Logic Model for the Office of Homeland Security Statistics

We developed an initial draft LM for OHSS, using the LM template shown in Figures A.1 and A.2, through the following processes:

- Review laws and policy providing relevant purpose information for OHSS. Evidence Act provisions were especially relevant in creating the LM. 5 U.S.C. § 314 calls on SOs to "advise on statistical procedures"; 44 U.S.C. § 3520 calls for SOs to perform a variety of CDO responsibilities related to compliance with statistical laws and to consult with CDOs on their management of data assets.
- Review existing OHSS plans and materials, including orders, charters, and introductory briefings.
- Review the proceedings of our interviews of OHSS's internal and external stakeholders.
- Review guidance for FSAs—most notably, the National Academies' *Principles and Practices for a Federal Statistical Agency.*[1]

This first LM was, by definition, highly limited in its inputs; it was intended strictly as an initial point of discussion for stakeholders to review and modify. The main vehicle we used for stakeholder input and refinement was a workshop.

## A Workshop to Support the Office of Homeland Security Statistics Logic Model Development

As discussed in Chapter 4, on November 1, 2023, we held a daylong workshop to

- obtain feedback from component-level SOs and similar officials to inform the operational LM and target operating model for the new OHSS, including its activities, outputs, and contributions to intended outcomes
- identify next steps for continuing to develop the OHSS models
- facilitate ongoing dialogue on the role of the new OHSS.[2]

The workshop was specifically designed to elicit feedback and enable discussions between OHSS stakeholders and statistical office SMEs. The workshop design included background about project purpose, an overview of key LM components, an explanation of the McKinsey 7-S framework, and two interactive breakout sessions to explore existing and future inputs, outputs, and outcomes necessary to position OHSS and OIS as efficient and effective organizations.

---

[1] CNSTAT, 2021.

[2] We led the workshop and conducted it under the Chatham House Rule:

> When a meeting, or part thereof, is held under the Chatham House Rule, participants are free to use the information received, but neither the identity nor the affiliation of the speaker(s), nor that of any other participant, may be revealed. (Chatham House, "Chatham House Rule," webpage, undated)

### Logic Model Exploration Design

The first breakout session focused on deconstructing necessary inputs, activities, outputs, stakeholders, intermediate outputs, outcomes, and organizational purpose to elicit issues, proposed changes, and potential metrics from the stakeholders. Table 4.1 in Chapter 4 defines the key components of the presented LM.

Table A.1 shows the exemplar questions workshop facilitators used to coordinate stakeholder discussions.

Based on the results of the workshop, Figure 4.1 in Chapter 4 shows an LM for OHSS. For further details on the results, see Chapter 4.

## Performance Measures Related to the Logic Model

### Quality and General Performance

The ICSP Program Assessment Rating Tool performance dimensions provide a core set of six performance measures covering both statistical product quality and general office performance. Figure A.3 shows the definitions of these measures and the elements of the OHSS LM to which they apply. As shown, most apply to OHSS's outputs, with the overarching mission achievement measure assessing stakeholders' intermediate outputs and outcomes.

Participants suggested that, during OHSS planning, the statistical product quality measures and metrics reflect the AORTAS acronym.

### Adherence to Principles for a Federal Statistical Agency

An additional set of measures has to do with standards of practice: adherence to generally accepted principles for an FSA. As captured in the National Academies' *Principles and Practices for a Federal Statistical Agency*, these are

- relevance to policy issues and society
- credibility among data users and stakeholders
- trust among the public and data providers
- independence from political and other undue influence
- continual improvement and innovation.[3]

[3] CNSTAT, 2021, pp. 2–4.

**TABLE A.1**

### Exemplar Questions for Logic Model Workshop Discussions

| Question | Further Probe |
|---|---|
| What should OHSS do? | • What activities should OHSS undertake?<br>• Do you see an immediate or future need for any specific activities (e.g., related to data governance, data management, data analytics, or support and training)?<br>• How could those activities help you address your biggest data problems or needs? |
| What should OHSS produce? | • What outputs, including services, should OHSS provide?<br>• Do you see an immediate or future need for any specific products (e.g., related to data governance, data management, data analytics, or support and training)? In this context, products could include statistical data, data catalogues, data dictionaries, statistical data standards, MOU templates, mediation services, analytical tools, or training materials.<br>• How could those products help you address your biggest data problems or needs?<br>• How would you expect to find, receive, or obtain the products? |

**FIGURE A.3**

### Interagency Committee on Standards Policy Performance Dimensions and Office of Homeland Security Statistics Logic Model Elements

| | | Measure | | |
|---|---|---|---|---|
| | | OHSS Outputs | OHSS Inputs | Stakeholders' Intermediate Outputs and Outcomes |
| Product quality | Relevance: Degree to which products and services are useful to users and responsive to users' needs | ✓ | | |
| | Accuracy: Correctness, validity, and reliability of data and products, by degree of closeness to target values | ✓ | | |
| | Timeliness: Assessment of the timing of information releases | ✓ | | |
| Program performance | Cost: Assessment of the dollar amount used to produce data products and services | ✓ | ✓ | |
| | Dissemination: Availability, accessibility, and distribution of products and services | ✓ | | |
| | Mission achievement: Effects of or satisfaction with statistical programs | | | ✓ |

SOURCE: Adapted from OMB, Executive Office of the President, "Strengthening Federal Statistics," *Analytical Perspectives: Budget of the United States Government, Fiscal Year 2009*, 2008a, Chart 4.1, p. 38.

# Overview of the Relevant Authorities

## Paperwork Reduction Act of 1995

According to OMB,

> [t]he PRA [Paperwork Reduction Act] makes OMB responsible, among other requirements, for coordination of the Federal Statistical System through an appointed Chief Statistician of the United States who is a trained and experienced professional statistician. The purpose of this coordination is to ensure the integrity, objectivity, impartiality, utility, and confidentiality of information collected for statistical purposes.[1]

## Information Quality Act of 2000

According to CIO.gov, "section 515 of [Appendix C of] Public Law 106-554, known as the Information Quality Act, required the [OMB] to promulgate guidance to agencies ensuring the quality, objectivity, utility, and integrity of information (including statistical information) disseminated by Federal agencies."[2] CRS also reported that the act "required agencies to issue their own information quality guidelines, and to establish administrative mechanisms that allow affected persons to seek correction of information maintained and disseminated by the agencies that does not comply with the OMB guidance."[3]

## Confidential Information Protection and Statistical Efficiency Act of 2018

According to OMB,

> CIPSEA 2002 established exclusively statistical uses of information collected under a pledge of confidentiality, provided for permitting controlled access to limited-use data through Designated Agent Agreements, and established strong penalties for willful violation of the confidentiality provisions, among other provisions. With enactment of the Evidence Act, CIPSEA 2018 codifies the uniform data protection requirements for Federal statistical collections, sets minimum standards for safeguarding confidential statistical data, and ensures the confidentiality of information collected exclusively for statistical purposes, in addition to numerous other provisions promoting safe and secure expanded access to restricted data. CIPSEA 2018 also: (1) codified the four fundamental responsibilities of statistical agencies and units and the role of other Federal agencies in supporting the statistical agencies and units to meet their responsibilities . . .; (2) required OMB to develop a process for recognizing additional statistical agencies and units; (3) pro-

---

[1] OMB, 2023, p. 56712 (we omitted a citation footnote that is present in the original); Public Law 96-511.

[2] U.S. Chief Information Officers Council, undated-a; Public Law 106-554, Appendix C, § 515.

[3] Copeland and Simpson, 2004, summary.

vided a presumption of accessibility to other Federal agencies' data for Recognized Statistical Agencies and Units; and (4) required a standard framework to allow expanding access to restricted data and establishment of a Standard Application Process.[4]

## Foundations for Evidence-Based Policymaking Act of 2018

The Evidence Act lists responsibilities for FSAs (labeled as "statistical agencies" in the statute), which are summarized in Table B.1.

**TABLE B.1**
**Statistical Agency Responsibilities in the Evidence Act**

| Category | Section of 44 U.S.C. | Responsibility |
|---|---|---|
| General | 3563(a)(1)(A) | "[P]roduce and disseminate relevant and timely statistical information" |
| | 3563(a)(1)(B) | "[C]onduct credible and accurate statistical activities" |
| | 3563(a)(1)(D) | "[P]rotect the trust of information providers by ensuring the confidentiality and exclusive statistical use of their responses" |
| Data protection | 3572(b) | "Data or information acquired by an agency under a pledge of confidentiality and for exclusively statistical purposes shall be used by officers, employees, or agents of the agency exclusively for statistical purposes and protected in accordance with such pledge." |
| | 3572(c)(1) | "Data or information acquired by an agency under a pledge of confidentiality for exclusively statistical purposes shall not be disclosed by an agency in identifiable form, for any use other than an exclusively statistical purpose, except with the informed consent of the respondent." |
| | 3572(c)(2) | "A disclosure pursuant to paragraph (1) is authorized only when the head of the agency approves such disclosure and the disclosure is not prohibited by any other law." |
| | 3572(d) | "A statistical agency or unit shall clearly distinguish any data or information it collects for nonstatistical purposes (as authorized by law) and provide notice to the public, before the data or information is collected, that the data or information could be used for nonstatistical purposes." |
| Data accessibility | 3581(a) | "The head of an agency shall, to the extent practicable, make any data asset maintained by the agency available, upon request, to any statistical agency or unit for purposes of developing evidence." |
| | 3582(a) | "To the extent practicable, each statistical agency or unit shall expand access to data assets of such agency or unit acquired or accessed under this subchapter to develop evidence while protecting such assets from inappropriate access and use, in accordance with the regulations promulgated under subsection (b)."<br>The statute also lists several requirements for these regulations and a standardized process by which individuals and organizations can apply for access to the data assets. |

NOTE: For data protection, these requirements apply to any agency that might request and receive information from individuals or organizations for statistical purposes. The law also should not be interpreted to restrict any other data confidentiality protections in other laws.

[4] OMB, 2023, pp. 56711–56712 (footnote omitted).

## Improving Statistical Activities Through Interagency Collaboration

M-15-15 is a July 2015 memorandum to selected executive branch agencies strongly encouraging interagency collaboration in the federal statistical community. It cites examples of how collaboration "has improved the quality of Federal statistical programs."[5] The memorandum also encourages the use of interagency procurement tools to better leverage resources.[6]

## Guidance for Providing and Using Administrative Data for Statistical Purposes

Issued in February 2014, M-14-06 is intended to provide "agencies with guidance for addressing the legal, policy, and operational issues that exist with respect to using administrative data for statistical purposes."[7] The memorandum has four stated elements:

> First the Memorandum calls for departmental and agency leadership to: (i) foster greater collaboration between program and statistical offices; (ii) develop strong data stewardship policies and practices around the statistical use of administrative data; (iii) require the documentation of quality control measures and key attributes of important administrative datasets; and (iv) require the designation of responsibilities and practices through the use of agreements amongst these offices.
>
> Second, the Memorandum encourages Federal departments and agencies to promote the use of administrative data for statistical purposes and provides guidance in addressing legal and policy requirements for such uses, including the need to continue to fully protect the privacy and confidentiality afforded to the individuals, businesses, and institutions providing the data.
>
> Third, the Memorandum also provides some "best practice" tools, including detailed guidance on the interaction of the Privacy Act requirements and the use of administrative data for statistical purposes, as well as a model interagency agreement for departments and agencies to follow when developing their policies and practices for sharing data for statistical purposes to another department or agency.[8]

## Phase 1 Implementation for Foundations for Evidence-Based Policymaking Act of 2018: Learning Agendas, Personnel, and Planning Guidance

The acting OMB director issued M-19-23 on July 10, 2019, to provide guidance to implement the requirements in the Evidence Act.[9] The memorandum summarizes the four phases of Evidence Act implementation:

- phase 1: learning agendas, personnel, and planning
- phase 2: open data access and management

---

5 Shelanski, 2015, p. 1.

6 Shelanski, 2015, p. 2.

7 Burwell, 2014, p. 2.

8 Burwell, 2014, p. 2.

9 Vought, 2019.

- phase 3: data access for statistical purposes
- phase 4: program evaluation.[10]

It focuses its guidance on phase 1 implementation. Most relevant to statistical agencies is Appendix C of the memorandum, which includes the responsibilities of SOs.

## Fundamental Responsibilities of Recognized Statistical Agencies and Units

Table B.2 describes relevant proposed sections of OMB's proposed rule.

TABLE B.2
**Proposed Rule by the Office of Management and Budget, Published on August 18, 2023, and Closed for Commentary on October 2, 2023**

| Proposed Section of Proposed Rule | Description |
|---|---|
| 1321.4(a) | Explains that a federal RSAU is responsible for fulfilling the fundamental responsibilities and requires that the parent agency support the RSAU's ability to meet its responsibilities |
| 1321.4(b) | Requires that a federal RSAU maintain a "distinctive, outward-facing website with its own domain name and with adequate control over the website content and management to uphold the fundamental responsibilities." (We have omitted a footnote from the original.) |
| 1321.4(b)(1) | Acknowledges that parent agency support is needed for an RSAU to develop and maintain an independent website, which includes ensuring availability of necessary resources |
| 1321.4(b)(2) | Indicates a website's importance in communicating key information to the public and requires an RSAU to have a strong mission statement that is also reflected in its strategic plan (assessed at least every four years) |
| 1321.4(c)(1) | Requires that an RSAU produce budget requests specific to its parent agency and "to participate directly . . . in presenting their agency specific request to OMB" |
| 1321.4(c)(2) | Requires that a parent agency "provide necessary resources or communicate to OMB through the Office of the Chief Statistician of the United States about the lack of available resources for Recognized Statistical Agencies or Units to carry out their fundamental responsibilities" |
| 1321.4(c)(3) | Requires that both an RSAU and its parent agency have sufficient staffing to ensure that the RSAU has necessary support services provided (e.g., IT) |
| 1321.4(c)(4) | Promotes collaboration between an RSAU and its parent agency on shared services |
| 1321.4(d) | Requires that an RSAU have appropriate decisionmaking authority |
| 1321.4(e)(1) | Directs that a parent agency review its policies to ensure that its RSAU can meet its statutory requirements |
| 1321.4(e)(2) | Requires consideration of an RSAU when its parent agency develops a new policy or regulation |
| 1321.4(e)(3) | Notes that an RSAU must be allowed to issue timely corrections and updates to statistical products |
| 1321.4(f) | Requires that OMB coordinate federal information policy in conjunction with the Evidence Act |
| 1321.5(a) | Requires that an RSAU produce relevant and timely statistics |
| 1321.5(b) | Requires that an RSAU be knowledgeable about its issue area, including about changes in policies and programs; indicates that the RSAU should engage with external stakeholders and be able to manage external relationships (such as with ACs) without undue influence from its parent agency |

[10] Vought, 2019, p. 3.

## Table B.2—Continued

| Proposed Section of Proposed Rule | Description |
|---|---|
| 1321.5(c) | Requires that an RSAU minimize the time between collection of data and release of statistical products |
| 1321.5(d) | Requires a release calendar for statistical products |
| 1321.6(a)(1) | Requires that an RSAU develop policies on the quality of its information and statistical products |
| 1321.6(a)(2) | Requires that an RSAU publish information on data collection methods, limitations, and sources of error |
| 1321.6(a)(3) | Requires that an RSAU comply with OMB standards and guidance for life-cycle data management practices |
| 1321.6(a)(4) | Requires that an RSAU ensure that its staff adhere to OMB peer-review policies |
| 1321.6(b)(1) | Establishes that an RSAU has sole authority for oversight of the quality of its statistical products |
| 1321.6(b)(3) | Prohibits all but an individual designated by an RSAU from making public comments on data released by that RSAU until after the official release of the data |
| 1321.6(b)(4) | Requires that a parent agency allow its RSAU to determine how products are released |
| 1321.6(b)(5) | Requires that a parent agency allow its RSAU to oversee its staff's participation in peer-review and professional development activities |
| 1321.7(a)(1) | Adopts a requirement that an RSAU "produce data that are impartial, clear, and complete and readily perceived as such by the public" |
| 1321.7(a)(2) | Adopts the provision that data be available on an equitable, policy-neutral, transparent, timely, and punctual basis |
| 1321.7(a)(3) | Adopts a requirement that an RSAU avoid even the appearance of potential interference from the parent agency and requires the RSAU to have staff trained in statistical methodology |
| 1321.7(a)(4) | Adopts a requirement that an RSAU "function in an environment that is clearly separate and autonomous from the other administrative, regulatory, law enforcement, or policymaking activities within their respective Departments," and clarifies that "functional separation" is not a prohibition on a parent agency articulating data needs to its RSAU |
| 1321.7(b)(1) | Prohibits a parent agency from requiring prior clearance of statistical products |
| 1321.7(b)(2) | Requires that a parent agency ensure that its RSAU can determine and carry out methods of conducting statistical activities for statistical purposes |
| 1321.7(b)(3) | Requires that, to the extent necessary to comply with statistical laws, the responsibility granted to a CDO for data governance and life-cycle data management be delegated in writing to the head of an RSAU; the CDO shall defer to the head of the RSAU |
| 1321.7(b)(4) and (5) | Requires that a parent agency allow its RSAU to manage resources to conduct objective statistical activities |
| 1321.8(a)(1) | Requires that an RSAU secure all confidential statistical data |
| 1321.8(a)(2) | Requires that an RSAU ensure that confidential statistical data are not used for nonstatistical purposes |
| 1321.8(a)(3) and (4) | Require that an RSAU communicate policies and procedures for ensuring confidentiality |
| 1321.8(a)(5) | Requires that an RSAU maintain and develop professional staff who are trained in statistical disclosure limitation and restricted access mechanisms |
| 1321.8(a)(6) | Requires that an RSAU inform employees, contractors, and other agents of the legal requirements to protect confidential statistical data and the associated penalties of disclosing such data |
| 1321.8(b)(1) | Requires that a parent agency ensure that its RSAU has sole authority to determine access to confidential statistical data |

**Table B.2—Continued**

| Proposed Section of Proposed Rule | Description |
|---|---|
| 1321.8(b)(2) | Requires that a parent agency implement Federal Information Technology Acquisition Reform Act authorities (the goal of which is to eliminate duplication and waste in IT acquisition)[a] |
| 1321.8(b)(3) | Seeks to ensure that a parent agency enable, support, and facilitate its RSAU in meeting its obligations in terms of privacy for information provided by respondents |

SOURCE: Features information from OMB, 2023, p. 56715.

[a] The Federal Information Technology Acquisition Reform Act is Public Law 113-291, Carl Levin and Howard P. "Buck" McKeon National Defense Authorization Act for Fiscal Year 2015, Title VIII, Acquisition Policy, Acquisition Management, and Related Matters; Subtitle D, Federal Information Technology Acquisition Reform, December 19, 2014, Title VIII, Subtitle D.

## Office of Management and Budget Directives

### Directive 1: Fundamental Responsibilities of Federal Statistical Agencies and Recognized Statistical Units

According to OMB,

> OMB's Directive No. 1 . . . articulates the four fundamental responsibilities of Recognized Statistical Agencies and Units and defines the requirements governing the design, collection, processing, editing, compilation, storage, analysis, release, and dissemination of statistical information by Recognized Statistical Agencies and Units.[11]

### Directive 2: Standards and Guidelines for Statistical Surveys

According to OMB,

> OMB's Statistical Policy Directive No. 2: Standards and Guidelines for Statistical Surveys describes specific practices that support the quality of design, collection, processing, production, analysis, review, and dissemination of information from statistical surveys.[12]

### Directive 3: Compilation, Release, and Evaluation of Principal Federal Economic Indicators

According to OMB,

> OMB's Statistical Policy Directive No. 3: Compilation, Release, and Evaluation of Principal Federal Economic Indicatorsestablishes requirements for Federal agencies regarding the compilation, release, and evaluation of statistical series designated by OMB as Principal Federal Economic Indicators, which are influential and heavily relied upon economic activity measures, including Gross Domestic Product, Consumer Price Index, and the Employment Situation.[13]

[11] OMB, 2023, p. 56712; OMB, 2014.

[12] OMB, 2023, p. 56712 (we have omitted a footnote that was present in the original); OMB, 2006.

[13] OMB, 2023, p. 56712 (we have omitted a footnote that was present in the original); OIRA, 2024a.

## Directive 4: Release and Dissemination of Statistical Products Produced by Federal Statistical Agencies

According to OMB,

> OMB's Statistical Policy Directive No. 4: Release and Dissemination of Statistical Products Produced by Federal Statistical Agencies establishes requirements for Recognized Statistical Agencies and Units on the release and dissemination of all statistical products, beyond just the Principal Federal Economic Indicators. Recognized Statistical Agencies and Units are required to follow these Directives to ensure that their release of information is equitable across all users, policy-neutral, transparent and understandable to the public, and timely to the needs of data users.[14]

## Directive 15: Standards for Maintaining, Collecting, and Presenting Federal Data on Race and Ethnicity

OMB initially developed Statistical Policy Directive (SPD) 15 in 1977 to "provide consistent data on race and ethnicity (when aggregated to the minimum reporting categories) throughout the Federal government, including the decennial census, household surveys, and Federal administrative forms."[15] As of the drafting of this report, SPD 15 was undergoing a formal review with the goal of issuing a revised SPD 15 by summer 2024.[16] In the interim, OMB issued its memorandum "Flexibilities and Best Practices for Implementing the Office of Management and Budget's 1997 Standards for Maintaining, Collecting, and Presenting Federal Data on Race and Ethnicity" to "implement SPD 15 for information collections which include measurements of race and ethnicity."[17]

## U.S. Department of Homeland Security Delegation 23037: Delegation to the Executive Director of the Office of Homeland Security Statistics

The delegation confers authority from the Under Secretary for Strategy, Policy, and Plans to the executive director of OHSS "to perform homeland security statistical activities and independent statistical reporting for the Department."[18]

---

[14] OMB, 2023, p. 56712 (we have omitted a footnote that was present in the original); OMB, 2008b.

[15] OMB, 2022, p. 3; OIRA, 2024b.

[16] OMB, 2022.

[17] OMB, 2022, p. 1.

[18] Silvers, 2023.

# Candidate Personae and Scenarios for Stakeholder Engagement

This appendix supplements Chapter 5. The proposed personae, described in Table C.1, are all fictitious people.

## Scenario Development

The purpose of scenarios as paired with personae is to create a compelling and relatable narrative to communicate how each persona fares through different futures. Potential futures are presented below. These scenarios and associated personae can form the basis for a future OHSS workshop and related strategy execution or policy development.

### Scenario Templates

We developed four scenario templates:

- A. More of the same but better
- B. More of the same but worse
- C. Different but worse (decay and depression)
- D. Different but better (fundamental change).

#### What Are the Key Questions for Office of Homeland Security Statistics Scenarios?

Mission: Maximize DHS data quality, transparency, and consistency; support data-driven decisionmaking; and improve the efficiency of statistical reporting.

- Q1: What organizational elements (e.g., roles, tasks, deliverables) are most critical to the daily operations of OHSS?
- Q2: What does a broadly successful OHSS look like?
- Q3: What does it look like if OHSS struggles in its mission?
- Q4: What would be the result of radical, positive changes to OHSS's purpose and activities?
- Q5: What is the absolute worst case for OHSS from a strategic perspective?

##### Scenario A: More of the Same but Better

OHSS succeeds at its mission, providing DHS and its components with valuable statistical information to drive department decisions. Other organizations find OHSS's products convenient and timely as well, using them to guide their own strategic thinking. There is universal trust that OHSS as an organization operates in the public interest.

TABLE C.1
## Personae and Scenarios for Stakeholder Engagement

| Persona Element | Persona | | | | | |
|---|---|---|---|---|---|---|
| | Consume Only | Command–Collaborate | Command–Consume | Collaborate–Consume 1 | Collaborate–Consume 2 | Command–Collaborate–Consume |
| Name | Emmy Wu | Melissa E. Walton | Malik Khan | Alfonso H. Parks | Desiree Wilson | Erin Ortega |
| Job title | Senior adviser for policy and advocacy | Analyst | U.S. Senate aide, majority | Statistician (General Schedule employee) | Program manager | Information-sharing and service analyst |
| Organization | Project NGO | SSP | U.S. Senate Committee on Agriculture, Nutrition, and Forestry Subcommittee on Rural Development and Energy | DHS Office of Uncrewed Underwater Vehicle Security, Statistical Unit | National Iris-Capture System Directorate | DHS OCIO |
| Goals | Work with congressional staff and committees to contribute information on issues related to bills and resolutions that are relevant to Project NGO advocacy objectives. Explore opportunities for congressional hearings and briefings relevant to issues of concern. | Enact delegated responsibilities from OMB to coordinate the FSS. | Assist subcommittee staff in performing office duties, conduct research, analyze legislation, draft memorandums, and assist in hearing preparation. | Inform DHS decisionmakers and help DHS fulfill its missions, collect data and information on operational activities. | Collect iris data and information to screen for threats attempting to enter the United States. | Implement the programs necessary to align DHS's IT personnel, resources, and assets. |

**Table C.1—Continued**

| Persona Element | Persona: Consume Only | Command–Collaborate | Command–Consume | Collaborate–Consume 1 | Collaborate–Consume 2 | Command–Collaborate–Consume |
|---|---|---|---|---|---|---|
| Purpose | Produce data-backed perspectives and position papers that support Project NGO interests. | In accordance with Title 44 of the U.S. Code, establish institutions and procedures through statutory provision. Manage the ICSP. Appoint the CSOTUS. | Draft legislation involving renewable-energy production and energy-efficiency improvement on farms and ranches and in rural communities; food and agricultural research, education, economics and extension; and innovation in the use of agricultural commodities and materials. | Identify specific statistical research areas that merit investigation, develop new hypotheses and approaches for studies, and evaluate the feasibility of such endeavors. Assess the adequacy and quality of data used in analyses. Prepare an explanation of the methodologies, results, and relevance of issues and problems under study. Disseminate results of research projects in a wide variety of venues, including publications, peer-reviewed journals, summaries, manuscripts, and special reports. Supervise and perform scientific work in applying statistical theories, techniques, and methods to gather, analyze, interpret, and report quantified information. | Maintain the data and security of national collection and analysis systems. Coordinate with other DHS and intelligence community entities to screen for known or suspected terrorists. Protect sensitive and classified data and information collected as part of the directorate's mission. | Establish DHS policies and guidance on data management. Protect DHS networks, systems, functions, and data. Enhance DHS business resilience and operational effectiveness. |

**Table C.1—Continued**

| Persona Element | Persona | | | | | |
|---|---|---|---|---|---|---|
| | Consume Only | Command–Collaborate | Command–Consume | Collaborate–Consume 1 | Collaborate–Consume 2 | Command–Collaborate–Consume |
| Challenges | Accurate data and relevant reports are difficult to find quickly and in easily accessible formats. | Various FSAs represent broad constituencies and diverse sets of statistical data. Ensuring confidentiality of data is difficult while maintaining their usefulness. Combining data from multiple sources to create more-useful data assets is difficult while protecting privacy. Artificial intelligence and machine learning are needed to support complex data analysis. | Quick turnarounds are needed on data requests. They might not fully know what data or information would be most useful for each request. | Developing project recommendations requires the application of technical and administrative judgment. Writing procedures for automated or computer-assisted statistical operations is difficult. Also difficult are selecting and applying advanced statistical techniques to experimental design, data analysis, sampling, forecasting, quality control, and operations research to resolve novel or obscure problems. | There is no memorandum of agreement with OHSS to allow data coordination. Protection of sensitive and classified data elements is difficult without OHSS having access to necessary systems. | Collaboration with OHSS on the management and security of statistical data is difficult. |
| Information they need | Timely public reports and public-use datasets on homeland security issues | DHS data standards, policies, and processes for ensuring accuracy of DHS metrics and statistical data provided to Congress | Congressionally mandated reports; briefings by DHS SMEs and responses to committee letters and questions; DHS-issued public reports | DHS data standards; DHS-preferred statistical practices; the DHS enterprise statistical system of record | DHS data standards; DHS-preferred statistical practices; the DHS enterprise statistical system of record; coordination efforts involving multiple components; guidance on and enforcement of DHS statistical standards[a] | DHS data standards; internal controls and authority to operate in the DHS enterprise statistical system of record |
| Information they provide | None | Standing up and updating OMB directives relevant to the FSS; coordination, guidance, and oversight for FSAs and their activities | Legislation that could affect the operations of one or more DHS SOs and OHSS; recommendations on funding allocation necessary for statistical agencies to address ongoing and future priorities | Component-specific statistical data, tools, and analysis; institutional knowledge relevant to past statistical interpretations and challenges unique to their component | Operational data in unclassified form | DHS IT policies and procedures; data management and security guidance |

[a] OHSS will likely not engage with classified data but will provide standards and learn what unclassified data might be of use for classified analyses and operations.

### Scenario B: More of the Same but Worse

OHSS struggles to accomplish its mission, which some in DHS view as irrelevant. The office struggles to obtain data from components. The components do not collectively follow OHSS-set standards, resulting in an inadequate statistical system of record. Its budget is diminished by competing PLCY demands.

### Scenario C: Different but Worse

The public and other stakeholders see OHSS as not independent, objective, or trustworthy, unnecessarily collecting personal data for unknown reasons. In reality, because processes are slow and overly burdensome and quality is inconsistent, decisionmakers mostly ignore OHSS data and reports except to support often-predetermined courses of action. Most of its reports are not made public because the data are sensitive and DHS leadership limits dissemination.

### Scenario D: Different but Better

OHSS is at the heart of a new way of thinking about statistical relevance. Its products are applied to national, regional, and local challenges in unique and beneficial ways that result in a more secure homeland. Various groups eagerly use statistical data and reporting to shape their own behaviors in ways that increase equity and improve quality of life.

# The McKinsey 7-S Factors

This appendix supplements Chapter 6 and provides generic considerations of the 7-S factors that could be applied to any organization.

## Shared Values

An organization's shared values are the beliefs and opinions held collectively by the people in the organization. These values and beliefs might differ from those held by individual members of the organization, but, in a healthy organization, individual values are generally aligned with those of the group. Because the intangibility of values means that they cannot be directly observed, they are often revealed through the examination of written, spoken, and symbolic artifacts or through the observation of individual and group behaviors. Their intangibility also means that extra care must be taken to effectively communicate what the desired values are. Whether positive or negative, as expressed by whether they support the organization's purpose and activities, the shared values guide the day-to-day behaviors of the organization's members. Like an organization's style, the organization's initial values are set by its founders. However, because of the constant influence of the beliefs, decisions, and behaviors of every member of the organization, the dynamic shifts as an organization grows and develops. If the desired values are not the ones being continuously reinforced, the organization's shared values will skew. This reinforcement can take the form of, for example, reminders, modeling by leaders, and reference in performance management programs. A healthy organization possesses an alignment between three facets of its shared values:

- The stated organizational values are aligned with the perceived organizational values.
- Individuals' values and beliefs are aligned with those of the organization, at least broadly.
- The organizational values are aligned with the organization's purpose and goals.

## Skills

An organization's capabilities often provide the best way of describing who it is by focusing on what it does. For an organization to enact its purpose effectively, it must establish or otherwise procure and maintain a pool of skills in its members. Organizational skills can also be maintained collectively within an organization, especially when they are regularly reinforced through performance criticality or frequent need. The exact set of skills that an organization needs and their distribution among the organization's members will vary over time; changes to each of the other 7-S factors are likely to result in the need for new skills, adjustments to existing skills, or the phasing out of skills that have become unnecessary. Individual members of a group are responsible for their own skills and their relation to current and anticipated task performance. The group's management is responsible for overseeing the collective skills of the group and for helping group members gain or improve their skills over time. To manage critical skills, the organization might need to monitor the group's conduct or assess skill performance against previously established and well-communicated standards. Besides closing any identified underskilling and skill gaps necessary to complete tasks, management also identifies skills that represent strengths of individuals and the team. These strengths can be a source of pride for the team and can become useful as the organization and its situations transform over time.

## Style

An organization's management and leadership styles should be distinct but complementary manifestations of the same organizational culture. The patterns of actions that managers exhibit translate an organization's purpose into the daily beliefs and behaviors of its members, whether that translation is accurate or not. An organization's members have a keen awareness of which functions, stakeholder relationships, subordinate teams, and so forth to which an organization's management applies its time and attention.[1] Members are also aware of the values revealed by their leaders and managers. They will reflect those values in their own behaviors and concentrate their efforts on the same organizational elements, ultimately directing the organization's performance. For that performance to be effective, the organization's leadership and management styles must align the vision and purpose of the organization with the daily conduct of its tasks and deliverables. Although style is the most intangible of the 7-S factors, it manifests in several ways that can be monitored and leveraged to prevent cultural misalignment. Clear definitions of the organization's values are easier for leaders and managers to implement and easier to understand in practice.[2] Formal and informal conversations, meetings, and other information-exchange opportunities are good times to reference the organization's vision, purpose, goals, and so on in writing with other members. In addition to their written messaging, managers and leaders must set the example through their actions to show they have bought into the mission and their teams' ability to accomplish it. Common behavioral markers of positive organizations include providing opportunities for members to engage with decisions and improvement initiatives, encouraging professional conflict while discouraging interpersonal conflict, and highlighting occasions for healthy competition and cooperation among members and groups within the organization.

## Staff

A staff—that is, all the members of an organization—is crucial to accomplishing that organization's mission. Commonly collected under the heading of *human resources* but with heavy engagement from the organization's management team, an organization's functions in relation to its staff include selection, allocation, engagement, reward, development, and protection. An organization's need for people with specific KSAs drives its acquisition of a suitable staff. The fundamental technique for determining an organization's staff needs is a job analysis, which identifies the human requirements of jobs and the context in which those jobs occur.[3] For many jobs, the direct supervisor is in the best position to define the duties and responsibilities, minimum qualifications, and expected levels of interaction with stakeholders. A commonly used format such as KSAs to describe each job's critical factors supports the implementation of less subjective candidate selection and performance management criteria. Additional segments of the job analysis outline the impact and decision authority awarded to the person holding the job, and to what degree they will have supervision

[1] Waterman, Peters, and Phillips, 1980.

[2] Waterman, Peters, and Phillips, 1980.

[3] U.S. Office of Personnel Management, undated.

of other members of the organization. Finally, the job analysis should contain a general idea of appropriate developmental activities, potential promotion pathways, and level of compensation for the job. Once the job analyses have been completed for the whole organization or a discrete portion of it, key roles or capability gaps may be identified that require the creation of additional jobs or the implementation of supplemental risk management measures to ensure effective operation.

## Structure

There is no single ideal structure because the best structure for an organization is informed by that organization's size, complexity, type of work, flexibility, attitude toward risk, etc. The structure of an organization is the most visible of the 7-S factors, usually through organizational charts and other diagrams.[4] Structural considerations traditionally receive an outsized amount of attention as an organization is formed or changes are made to it. In fact, the McKinsey 7-S framework was developed primarily to portray important elements of organizational change other than just structure. Although an important factor for the organization, its structure serves only two major functions—dividing labor and coordinating between disparate components.[5] Division of labor includes the establishment of partitions within the organization aligned according to certain areas of knowledge, processes, and tools for efficiency and ease of management. A balance must be struck between decentralization of control for better communication within the partitions and centralization for increased unity of effort. The more that an organization divides its labor, the more coordination is required to maintain cohesiveness. If the organization is too divided, the coordination function becomes too onerous to be effective. The equilibrium between specialization and integration tasks is another way that organizations determine this balance. Various mapping formats are used to establish the needs of an organization's structure, such as where assets are physically located, how information flows, how materials flow, and where and by whom decisions are made. Some of the relevant structural data might also be combined into a single graphic.

## Strategy

Strategy is ultimately a plan for how an organization will respond to external changes. For public-sector organizations, strategy is less critical than for private-sector entities in that competition and market share have less meaning. Instead, strategies for nonprofits and government agencies should focus on the organizational performance expected of them, provide a common direction around which the organization's members can rally, respond to stakeholder demands, and present a professional approach to achieving its purpose.[6] Regardless of the type of organization, strategies serve to encourage the long-term sustainability of the organization so that it can continue to achieve its purpose. To align a strategic plan with the other 7-S framework factors, experts have recommended that a combination of analysis and intuition be applied. For instance, organizational performance mandates or expectations might be explicitly documented by statutory, regulatory, or other guidance. On the other hand, performance goals could be identified by any member of the organization with sufficient understanding of its shared values, skills, and systems. A strategic plan

---

4 Waterman, Peters, and Phillips, 1980.

5 Waterman, Peters, and Phillips, 1980

6 Isaiah O. Ugboro, Kofi Obeng, and Ora Spann, "Strategic Planning as an Effective Tool of Strategic Management in Public Sector Organizations: Evidence from Public Transit Organizations," *Administration and Society*, Vol. 43, No. 1, January 2011.

should be built on a suitable analysis of the best data available to the organization while leaving enough flexibility in its implementation to allow leaders and managers to make decisions relevant to changes in environmental factors. A strategy that lacks this ability will actually work against the organization's effectiveness by not allowing the organization to reprioritize its ways and means so that it can continue to make progress toward strategic goals.[7] Especially in times marked by instability and upheaval, an adaptable strategy will allow the organization to make small gains while other organizations come to a standstill.[8] This characteristic of constancy through resilience and adaptability engenders stakeholder trust in the organization, which is crucial for public institutions.

## Systems

After structure, systems are the most visible 7-S factor of an organization. Depending on the formality of the organization, systems might be well documented in policies, SOPs, desktop procedures, process maps, job aids, and other formats. Processes are the most-common organizational systems, along with their supporting procedures. Some software tools might also be defined as systems if they are used to produce outputs for internal or external stakeholders. Back-office systems related to the organization's functioning and operational systems related to its performance are both critical to the organization, and manifestations of systems within the other 7-S factors are manifold.[9] Systems can be defined at any level of the organization for which they are useful, from the individual to the entirety of the organization. Many systems will be of central importance to one or two subdivisions but have an influence on others. These points of interaction are often sites of process failure, miscommunication, and lack of interoperability; being intentional about the design of each system can support positive integration across individuals, teams, and functions at these points. One common approach to system design and modification is the use of mapping, such as input–process–output diagrams, to describe the basic structure of a process. Diagramming the inputs, outputs, and tasks associated with each process makes it easier to identify organizational shortfalls that result in degraded performance.[10] Some more information-dense versions of the input–process–output diagram include turtle diagrams that also identify resource and personnel requirements, documentation of methods, and performance indicators, while still others incorporate feedback mechanisms. Whichever style of system map is used, its level of formality and detail will be determined by the needs of the organization; different departments or functions might use different styles that better match their needs. In cases in which different styles are used, special attention must be paid to the systems that cross these borders, as discussed previously, to ensure that the systems are fit for use by their users.

---

[7] Ugboro, Obeng, and Spann, 2011.

[8] Zincir and Tunç, 2017.

[9] Waterman, Peters, and Phillips, 1980.

[10] Annie Millar, Ronald S. Simeone, and John T. Carnevale, "Logic Models: A Systems Tool for Performance Management," *Evaluation and Program Planning*, Vol. 24, No. 1, February 2001.

APPENDIX E

# Interview Protocols

## The Federal Statistical Agency Interview Protocol

### Background

RAND is assisting the Secretary of Homeland Security in expanding OIS into an independent FSA): OHSS. Our team is helping DHS develop an organizational strategy and implementation plan for OHSS.

Toward that end, we'd like to learn from you. You all are the experts on FSAs, and we'd appreciate any lessons learned, pitfalls to avoid, specific challenges to prepare for, and the benefits of FSAs for their host departments.

We've already completed a survey of DHS's and the FSAs' statistical activities—at least what is available publicly. The purpose of today's discussion is to help us better understand your organization: What are the lessons you've learned about how to run an FSA, mistakes to avoid, and stakeholders to engage?

I don't expect that we'll need to worry about this, but please note that this is an *unclassified* interview. Do not discuss classified information in your responses. If you would like to have a classified follow-up discussion with us on a topic, just let us know and we can arrange it.

### Voluntary Participation

Participation is entirely voluntary. If you do agree to participate, you are not required to answer every question. If at any time you do not want to answer a question or would like to stop the interview, please let us know. There are no penalties for doing so.

### Confidentiality

We will take notes during the interview to have a record of what was discussed about OHSS. We will keep your information confidential, which means we will not cite participants by name or attribute select comments to individuals; however, we will acknowledge that we spoke with categories of people. It is possible, though unlikely, that someone who reads the report could infer who provided a statement or quote. If you have questions about your rights as a research participant or need to report a research-related concern, please contact RAND's Human Subjects Protection Committee toll-free at (866) 697-5620 or by emailing hspcinfo@rand.org.

Do we have your permission to record the transcript of this discussion?

### For More Information

For questions about the study, please contact the project leaders, Elina Treyger (Elina_Treyger@rand.org), Douglas Ligor (Douglas_Ligor@rand.org), and Joseph Chang (Joseph_Chang@rand.org).

## Big Questions

- We'd like to get know *you*. What's your position, and what do you do? How long have you been at [FSA]?
- In your estimation, what are the essential principles and practices for an FSA?
  - Prompt around independence.
- What advice would you give OHSS (regarding setting up a new FSA)?
- What are big issues that [FSA] is facing next, or recent challenges that y'all have had to deal with?

## Relationship to Agency

- What is [FSA]'s position within [larger agency]? Where does [FSA] fit within the agency's structure?
- What is the relationship between your office and the agency's leadership? Do you report directly to [agency director]?
- How do you maintain independence and objectivity in your data collection and analysis? What directions or guidelines do you receive from [larger agency]?
  - Do you believe that your existing policy or guidance is sufficient for your mission?
- Do you conduct analysis or reporting for [larger agency], and how is that process managed?

## Resources and Personnel

- Do you set and have control over your own budgets?
  - **If no:** Are there any advantages to that?
  - **If no:** How do you maintain independence (if you do) in that circumstance?
- Are there other financial management challenges OHSS should be aware of or prepare for?
- How do you maintain a stable workforce?
  - What balance of full-time staff versus contractors do you use?
  - Are there any lessons learned in hiring, onboarding, and training that OHSS could benefit from?
  - Are there any particular emerging skill sets that an FSA should seek in the hiring process (e.g., data scientists)?

## Organizational Metrics

- What metrics does [FSA] use to measure its accuracy, impact, and efficacy? How were those metrics developed?
  - Are these metrics unique to your organization, or are they aligned with other departments or agencies in this space?
- What mechanisms do you have to obtain feedback?
- What processes are in place to implement organizational changes? How does [FSA] renew itself over time?
  - Has your office experienced any significant organizational changes?
    - [*If so*, did this restructure create any new enablers for your mission?]
- **If a "young" FSA:** Do you have any lessons learned specifically on rolling out or standing up a new FSA?
  - **Prompt:** What would a successful FSA rollout look like to you? An unsuccessful one?

### Stakeholders

- How did your office determine your principal stakeholders and audience?
- What practices would you recommend that FSAs do to generate buy-in for their mission with their audiences? With department management? With data-sending agencies?
- How do you gain their buy-in? Do you engage stakeholders on a regular basis? If so, how?
- Given the importance of independence and relevance, how would you recommend that officials and agencies balance requests from other parts of the department and departmental leadership?
- What should new statistical officials or agencies consider as they design plans for strategic engagement?

### Data Management

- How do you engage with other FSAs, statistical programs, and other statistical activities within your agency?
- What approaches has your office used for collecting data from other parts of your organization that manage operational datasets?
  - Are there any trade-offs between accessing data and maintaining independence?
- How do you go about gathering sensitive data that the data-sending agencies might not want to share?
- What is the impact of relying on sensitive data and information as they relate to trust and dissemination?

## The U.S. Department of Homeland Security Interview Protocol

### Background

RAND is assisting the Secretary of Homeland Security in expanding OIS into an independent statistical unit: OHSS. Our team is helping DHS develop an organizational strategy and implementation plan for OHSS.

As part of that, we are gathering information about your views on your component's statistical activities, the OHSS process, and how the latter will affect the former. In addition to consulting public sources, the Homeland Security Operational Analysis Center research team will be conducting two rounds of interviews with DHS subject-matter experts over the next several months. The team's goal for the first round of interviews is to understand any challenges and opportunities you may wish to share.

Please note that this is an *unclassified* interview. Do not discuss classified information in your responses. If you would like to have a classified follow-up discussion with us on a topic, just let us know and we can arrange it.

### Voluntary Participation

Participation is entirely voluntary. If you do agree to participate, you are not required to answer every question. If at any time you do not want to answer a question or would like to stop the interview, please let us know. There are no penalties for doing so.

### Confidentiality

We will take notes during the interview to have a record of what was discussed about OHSS. We will keep your information confidential, which means we will not cite participants by name or attribute select comments to individuals; however, we will acknowledge that we spoke with categories of people. It is possible, though unlikely, that someone who reads the report could infer who provided a statement or quote. If you have questions about your rights as a research participant or need to report a research-related concern, please contact RAND's Human Subjects Protection Committee toll-free at (866) 697-5620 or by emailing hspcinfo@rand.org.

Do we have your permission to record the transcript of this discussion?

## For More Information

For questions about the study, please contact the project leaders, Elina Treyger (Elina_Treyger@rand.org), Douglas Ligor (Douglas_Ligor@rand.org), and Joseph Chang (Joseph_Chang@rand.org).

## Component Alignment with the Office of Homeland Security Statistics

We're interested in understanding how you think a future OHSS will affect your component's missions, services, and data practices.

- Are there positives you hope this office might have for your component?
  - *Possible prompt:* Additional data collection, analytical services, FOIA offloading, public outreach?
- What about any concerns?
- Are there challenges your component will face in aligning its missions, functions, activities, etc., with this future office?
  - Internal statistical analysis that you conduct (that might be replaced or not provide the same service)?
  - Personnel, training, funding, etc.?
  - What could OHSS do to make this alignment easier for you?
- *Reserve prompt:* What would a successful OHSS rollout look like to you? An unsuccessful one?

## Security, Control, and Usage

OHSS is intended to establish a shared understanding of statistical data, analysis, and process. In particular, the leadership has defined statistical data as information that is anonymized and cannot be traced back to individuals. Also, OHSS will be a federal statistical agency, meaning that it will have some degree of independence in how it analyzes data and to whom it disseminates data.

- Will these functions pose any issues for your component?
  - How would they affect your statistical activities?
- Are there any steps OHSS could take to mitigate any concerns you might have?
- *Reserve prompt:* What criteria would you recommend that OHSS use to determine whether and how information should be publicly available?

## Internal Data-Sharing and Standardization

We previously conducted a project on how DHS uses data. Some interviewees expressed concern about the components' ability to share data with and obtain data from each other. A lot of this came down to questions of standardization—setting uniform definitions and usages of collected information.

- How do you think OHSS should navigate these problems?
- How would standardization at the OHSS level affect your statistical activities?
  - Are there certain activities you would conduct if you had access to other components' data?
  - Are there certain activities you'd have to discontinue?

## Others

- Are there any other questions or concerns we haven't asked about that you think we should know about?
- As DHS works to stand up OHSS, what are some lessons it might take from the experience of your agency in establishing and managing a federal statistical agency?
  - Do you have any other advice for those standing up OHSS?

# Abbreviations

| | |
|---|---|
| AC | advisory committee |
| AORTAS | accurate, objective, relevant, timely, accessible statistics |
| BEA | Bureau of Economic Analysis |
| BJS | Bureau of Justice Statistics |
| BLS | U.S. Bureau of Labor Statistics |
| BTS | Bureau of Transportation Statistics |
| CBP | U.S. Customs and Border Protection |
| CDO | chief data officer |
| CIPSEA | Confidential Information Protection and Statistical Efficiency Act |
| CISA | Cybersecurity and Infrastructure Security Agency |
| CNSTAT | Committee on National Statistics |
| CRS | Congressional Research Service |
| CSOTUS | chief statistician of the United States |
| DHS | U.S. Department of Homeland Security |
| DOJ | U.S. Department of Justice |
| DSSD | U.S. Department of Homeland Security statistical standards database |
| EIA | U.S. Energy Information Administration |
| ERS | Economic Research Service |
| FCSM | Federal Committee on Statistical Methodology |
| FEMA | Federal Emergency Management Agency |
| FLETC | Federal Law Enforcement Training Centers |
| FOIA | Freedom of Information Act |
| FSA | federal statistical agency |
| FSS | Federal Statistical System |
| FY | fiscal year |
| GAO | U.S. Government Accountability Office |
| I&A | Office of Intelligence and Analysis |
| ICE | U.S. Immigration and Customs Enforcement |
| ICSP | Interagency Council on Statistical Policy |
| IT | information technology |
| KSAs | knowledge, skills, and abilities |
| LM | logic model |
| LOE | line of effort |

| | |
|---|---|
| MOU | memorandum of understanding |
| NASS | National Agricultural Statistics Service |
| NCES | National Center for Education Statistics |
| NCHS | National Center for Health Statistics |
| NCSES | National Center for Science and Engineering Statistics |
| NGO | nongovernmental organization |
| OCIO | Office of the Chief Information Officer |
| OHSS | Office of Homeland Security Statistics |
| OIG | Office of Inspector General |
| OIRA | Office of Information and Regulatory Affairs |
| OIS | Office of Immigration Statistics |
| OMB | Office of Management and Budget |
| ORES | Office of Research, Evaluation, and Statistics |
| PLCY | Office of Strategy, Policy, and Plans |
| PSA | principal statistical agency |
| QA | quality assurance |
| QC | quality control |
| RFI | request for information |
| RSAU | recognized statistical agency or unit |
| SMART | specific, measurable, achievable, relevant, and time-bound |
| SME | subject-matter expert |
| SO | statistical official |
| SOI | Statistics of Income |
| SOP | standard operating procedure |
| SPD | statistical policy directive |
| SSP | Statistical and Science Policy |
| TSA | Transportation Security Administration |
| USCG | U.S. Coast Guard |
| USCIS | U.S. Citizenship and Immigration Services |
| USSS | U.S. Secret Service |

# References

Administrative Office of the U.S. Courts, "Statistics and Reports," webpage, undated. As of July 20, 2024: https://www.uscourts.gov/statistics-reports

Advisory Committee on Data for Evidence Building, Bureau of Economic Analysis, U.S. Department of Commerce, "The U.S. Federal Statistical System," briefing slides, January 22, 2021.

BEA—*See* Bureau of Economic Analysis.

BLS—*See* U.S. Bureau of Labor Statistics.

Brown, Tim, "Design Thinking," *Harvard Business Review*, June 2008.

BTS—*See* Bureau of Transportation Statistics.

Bureau of Economic Analysis, U.S. Department of Commerce, "Who We Are," webpage, last modified September 8, 2023. As of January 5, 2024:
https://www.bea.gov/about/who-we-are

Bureau of Economic Analysis Advisory Committee, Bureau of Economic Analysis, U.S. Department of Commerce, *Charter*, June 4, 2023.

Bureau of Transportation Statistics, U.S. Department of Transportation, "Advisory Council on Transportation Statistics," webpage, September 10, 2015. As of January 4, 2024:
https://www.bts.gov/acts

Burwell, Sylvia M., director, Office of Management and Budget, Executive Office of the President, "Guidance for Providing and Using Administrative Data for Statistical Purposes," memorandum for the heads of executive departments and agencies, Memorandum M-14-06, February 14, 2014.

Campbell, Andrew, "Brief Case: Strategy and Intuition—A Conversation with Henry Mintzberg," *Long Range Planning*, Vol. 24, No. 2, April 1991.

Chatham House, "Chatham House Rule," webpage, undated. As of July 20, 2024:
https://www.chathamhouse.org/about-us/chatham-house-rule

CIPSEA—*See* Public Law 107-347.

CIPSEA 2018—*See* Public Law 115-435, Title III.

Citro, Constance F., Jonathan Auerbach, Katherine Smith Evans, Erica L. Groshen, J. Steven Landefeld, Jeri Mulrow, Thomas Petska, Steve Pierson, Nancy Potok, Charles J. Rothwell, John Thompson, James L. Woodworth, and Edward Wu, "What Protects the Autonomy of the Federal Statistical Agencies? An Assessment of the Procedures in Place to Protect the Independence and Objectivity of Official U.S. Statistics," *Statistics and Public Policy*, Vol. 10, No. 1, 2023.

CNSTAT—*See* Committee on National Statistics.

Committee on National Statistics; Division of Behavioral and Social Sciences and Education; National Academies of Sciences, Engineering, and Medicine, *Principles and Practices for a Federal Statistical Agency*, 7th ed., National Academies Press, 2021.

Confidential Information Protection and Statistical Efficiency Act—*See* Public Law 107-347.

Copeland, Curtis W., and Michael Simpson, *The Information Quality Act: OMB's Guidance and Initial Implementation*, Congressional Research Service, RL32532, August 19, 2004.

DHS—*See* U.S. Department of Homeland Security.

European Statistical System Committee, *European Statistics Code of Practice*, rev. ed. 2017, endorsed November 16, 2017.

Evidence Act—*See* Public Law 115-435.

Federal Economic Statistics Advisory Committee, Office of the Under Secretary for Economic Affairs, U.S. Department of Commerce, *Charter*, September 27, 2022.

Federal Emergency Management Agency, U.S. Department of Homeland Security, "National Household Survey," webpage, last updated December 22, 2023. As of July 20, 2024:
https://www.fema.gov/about/openfema/data-sets/national-household-survey

Feinberg, Melanie, "The Myth of Objective Data," *MIT Press Reader*, April 17, 2023.

FEMA—*See* Federal Emergency Management Agency.

Foundations for Evidence-Based Policymaking Act of 2018—*See* Public Law 115-435.

Greenfield, Victoria A., Valerie L. Williams, and Elisa Eiseman, *Using Logic Models for Strategic Planning and Evaluation: Application to the National Center for Injury Prevention and Control*, RAND Corporation, TR-370-NCIPC, 2006. As of December 7, 2023:
https://www.rand.org/pubs/technical_reports/TR370.html

Hawes, Michael, and Sallie Keller, "What Do We Mean by 'For Statistical Purposes Only'?" Federal Committee on Statistical Methodology 2023 Research and Policy Conference, Session B-5, October 24, 2023.

Hayes, John, *The Theory and Practice of Change Management*, Palgrave Macmillan, 2014.

Interagency Council on Statistical Policy, "Charter of the Interagency Council on Statistical Policy Subcommittee on Statistical Official Roles and Responsibilities," approved and adopted February 7, 2024.

Jansen, Bernard J., Soon-gyo Jung, Dianne Ramirez Robillos, and Joni Salminen, "Too Few, Too Many, Just Right: Creating the Necessary Number of Segments for Large Online Customer Populations," *Electronic Commerce Research and Applications*, Vol. 49, September–October 2021.

Keller, Sallie Ann, and Michael B. Hawes, "Deciphering and Interpreting 'for Statistical Purposes,'" briefing presented at the Federal Committee on Statistical Methodology 2023 Research and Policy Conference, October 24, 2023.

M-14-06—*See* Burwell, "Guidance for Providing and Using Administrative Data for Statistical Purposes."

M-15-15—*See* Shelansky, "Improving Statistical Activities Through Interagency Collaboration."

M-19-23—*See* Vought, "Phase 1 Implementation of the Foundations for Evidence-Based Policymaking Act of 2018."

Masilela, Lucia, and Danielle Nel, "The Role of Data and Information Security Governance in Protecting Public Sector Data and Information Assets in National Government in South Africa," *Africa's Public Service Delivery and Performance Review*, Vol. 9, No. 1, 2021.

McKinsey and Company, "People and Organizational Performance," webpage, undated. As of August 27, 2024:
https://www.mckinsey.com/capabilities/people-and-organizational-performance/how-we-help-clients

Millar, Annie, Ronald S. Simeone, and John T. Carnevale, "Logic Models: A Systems Tool for Performance Management," *Evaluation and Program Planning*, Vol. 24, No. 1, February 2001.

Mintzberg, Henry, *The Rise and Fall of Strategic Planning: Reconceiving Roles for Planning, Plans, Planners*, Free Press, 1994.

NASS—*See* National Agricultural Statistics Service.

National Agricultural Statistics Service, U.S. Department of Agriculture, "About NASS," webpage, last modified May 4, 2018. As of January 5, 2024:
https://www.nass.usda.gov/About_NASS/Mission_Statement/index.php

National Agricultural Statistics Service, U.S. Department of Agriculture, "Surveys," webpage, last modified April 17, 2024. As of August 27, 2024:
https://www.nass.usda.gov/Surveys/Guide_to_NASS_Surveys/Dairy_Products/index.php

Office of Homeland Security Statistics, U.S. Department of Homeland Security, "About OHSS," webpage, undated. As of March 29, 2024:
https://www.dhs.gov/ohss/about-ohss

Office of Information and Regulatory Affairs, Office of Management and Budget, Executive Office of the President, "Order Providing for the Confidentiality of Statistical Information," *Federal Register*, Vol. 62, No. 124, June 27, 1997 (final order).

Office of Information and Regulatory Affairs, Office of Management and Budget, Executive Office of the President, "Update of Statistical Policy Directive No. 3: Compilation, Release, and Evaluation of Principal Federal Economic Indicators—Changing Timing of Public Comments by Employees of the Executive Branch," *Federal Register*, Vol. 89, No. 32, February 15, 2024a (notice of a revised Statistical Policy Directive 3).

Office of Information and Regulatory Affairs, Office of Management and Budget, Executive Office of the President, "Revisions to OMB's Statistical Policy Directive No. 15: Standards for Maintaining, Collecting, and Presenting Federal Data on Race and Ethnicity," *Federal Register*, Vol. 89, No. 62, March 29, 2024 (notice of decision).

Office of Information Policy, U.S. Department of Justice, "Create an Annual Report," webpage, undated. As of May 30, 2024:
https://www.foia.gov/data.html

Office of Management and Budget, Executive Office of the President, *Standards and Guidelines for Statistical Surveys*, Statistical Policy Directive 2, September 2006.

Office of Management and Budget, Executive Office of the President, "Implementation Guidance for Title V of the E-Government Act, Confidential Information Protection and Statistical Efficiency Act of 2002 (CIPSEA)," *Federal Register*, Vol. 72, No. 115, June 15, 2007 (notice of decision).

Office of Management and Budget, Executive Office of the President, "Strengthening Federal Statistics," *Analytical Perspectives: Budget of the United States Government, Fiscal Year 2009*, 2008a.

Office of Management and Budget, Executive Office of the President, "Statistical Policy Directive No. 4: Release and Dissemination of Statistical Products Produced by Federal Statistical Agencies," *Federal Register*, Vol. 73, No. 46, March 7, 2008b (notice of final decision).

Office of Management and Budget, Executive Office of the President, "Statistical Policy Directive No. 1: Fundamental Responsibilities of Federal Statistical Agencies and Recognized Statistical Units," *Federal Register*, Vol. 79, No. 231, December 2, 2014 (notice of final decision).

Office of Management and Budget, Executive Office of the President, *Statistical Programs of the United States Government: Fiscal Years 2019/2020*, December 11, 2020.

Office of Management and Budget, Executive Office of the President, "Flexibilities and Best Practices for Implementing the Office of Management and Budget's 1997 Standards for Maintaining, Collecting, and Presenting Federal Data on Race and Ethnicity," Statistical Policy Directive 15, July 2022.

Office of Management and Budget, Executive Office of the President, "Fundamental Responsibilities of Recognized Statistical Agencies and Units," *Federal Register*, Vol. 88, No. 159, August 18, 2023 (notice of proposed rulemaking).

Office of Management and Budget, Executive Office of the President, *Statistical Programs of the United States Government: Fiscal Years 2021/2022*, February 2024.

OHSS—*See* Office of Homeland Security Statistics.

OIRA—*See* Office of Information and Regulatory Affairs.

OMB—*See* Office of Management and Budget.

Organisation for Economic Co-operation and Development, *The OECD Privacy Framework*, 2013.

Organisation for Economic Co-operation and Development, "Recommendation of the Council on Good Statistical Practice," OECD/LEGAL/0417, adopted November 22, 2015, amended March 12, 2019.

Panel on Improving Federal Statistics for Policy and Social Science Research Using Multiple Data Sources and State-of-the-Art Estimation Methods; Committee on National Statistics; Division of Behavioral and Social Sciences and Education; National Academies of Sciences, Engineering, and Medicine, *Innovations in Federal Statistics: Combining Data Sources While Protecting Privacy*, National Academies Press, 2017.

Peters, Tom, "A Brief History of the 7-S ('McKinsey 7-S') Model," blog post, January 9, 2011. As of July 26, 2023:
https://tompeters.com/2011/03/a-brief-history-of-the-7-s-mckinsey-7-s-model/

Privacy Act—*See* Public Law 93-579.

Privacy Protection Study Commission, *Personal Privacy in an Information Society: The Report of the Privacy Protection Study Commission*, July 1977.

Public Law 77-507, an act to further expedite the prosecution of the war, March 27, 1942.

Public Law 89-487, an act to amend § 3 of the Administrative Procedure Act, Chapter 324, of the act of June 11, 1946, to clarify and protect the right of the public to information, July 4, 1966.

Public Law 93-579, Privacy Act of 1974, December 31, 1974.

Public Law 104-13, Paperwork Reduction Act of 1995, May 22, 1995.

Public Law 106-554, Consolidated Appropriations Act, 2001, December 21, 2000.

Public Law 107-56, Uniting and Strengthening America by Providing Appropriate Tools Required to Intercept and Obstruct Terrorism (USA PATRIOT) Act of 2001, October 26, 2001.

Public Law 107-296, Homeland Security Act of 2002, November 25, 2002.

Public Law 107-347, E-Government Act of 2002; Title V, Confidential Information Protection and Statistical Efficiency Act, December 17, 2002.

Public Law 113-291, Carl Levin and Howard P. "Buck" McKeon National Defense Authorization Act for Fiscal Year 2015, Title VIII, Acquisition Policy, Acquisition Management, and Related Matters; Subtitle D, Federal Information Technology Acquisition Reform, December 19, 2014.

Public Law 115-435, Foundations for Evidence-Based Policymaking Act of 2018, January 14, 2019.

Purple Book—*See* Committee on National Statistics, *Principles and Practices for a Federal Statistical Agency.*

Sah, Prakash, *Defining Enterprise Data and Analytics Strategy: Pragmatic Guidance on Defining Strategy Based on Successful Digital Transformation Experience of Multiple Fortune 500 and Other Global Companies*, Springer, 2022.

Selznick, Philip, *Leadership in Administration: A Sociological Interpretation*, University of California Press, 1957.

Shelanski, Howard, administrator, Office of Information and Regulatory Affairs, Office of Management and Budget, Executive Office of the President, "Improving Statistical Activities Through Interagency Collaboration," memorandum for the heads of selected executive departments and agencies, Memorandum M-15-15, July 8, 2015.

Silvers, Robert, Under Secretary, Office of Strategy, Policy, and Plans; U.S. Department of Homeland Security, "Establishing an Office of Homeland Security Statistics," memorandum for the Secretary, July 25, 2022.

Silvers, Robert, Under Secretary, Office of Strategy, Policy, and Plans; U.S. Department of Homeland Security, *Delegation to the Executive Director of the Office of Homeland Security Statistics*, Delegation 23037, revision 00, September 29, 2023.

Sivinski, Bob, chief statistician of the United States, "Statistical Purposes: United States and International Policy Framework," briefing presented at the Federal Committee on Statistical Methodology 2023 Research and Policy Conference, October 24, 2023.

StatsPolicy, "About Us," webpage, undated. As of January 4, 2024:
https://www.statspolicy.gov/about/

Ugboro, Isaiah O., Kofi Obeng, and Ora Spann, "Strategic Planning as an Effective Tool of Strategic Management in Public Sector Organizations: Evidence from Public Transit Organizations," *Administration and Society*, Vol. 43, No. 1, January 2011.

United Nations Statistics Division, "Principle 6: Confidentiality," *Fundamental Principles of Official Statistics*, A/RES/68/261, January 29, 2014.

U.S. Bureau of Labor Statistics, U.S. Department of Labor, "Technical Advisory Committee Charter," October 4, 2022a.

U.S. Bureau of Labor Statistics, U.S. Department of Labor, "Data Users Advisory Committee Charter," October 28, 2022b.

U.S. Census Bureau, U.S. Department of Commerce, "2030 Census Advisory Committee (2030 CAC)," webpage, last revised October 17, 2023. As of January 4, 2024:
https://www.census.gov/about/cac/2030cac.html

U.S. Chief Information Officers Council, "2.9 Information Quality Act (2000): Information Technology Laws," webpage, undated. As of July 20, 2024:
https://www.cio.gov/handbook/it-laws/information-quality-act/

U.S. Chief Information Officers Council, "2.11 Confidential Information Protection and Statistical Efficiency Act (2002): Information Technology Laws," webpage, undated. As of July 20, 2024:
https://www.cio.gov/handbook/it-laws/cipsea/

U.S. Code, Title 5, Government Organization and Employees; Part I, The Agencies Generally; Chapter 3, Powers; Subchapter II, Federal Evidence-Building Activities; Section 314, Statistical Expertise.

U.S. Code, Title 6, Domestic Security; Chapter 1, Homeland Security Organization; Subchapter III, Science and Technology in Support of Homeland Security; Section 185, Federally Funded Research and Development Centers.

U.S. Code, Title 13, Census.

U.S. Code, Title 44, Public Printing and Documents; Chapter 35, Coordination of Federal Information Policy.

U.S. Department of Homeland Security, *DHS Sensitive Systems*, Policy Directive 4300A, version 13.1, July 17, 2017.

U.S. Department of Homeland Security, "FOIA Annual Reports," webpage, last updated March 25, 2024. As of July 20, 2024:
https://www.dhs.gov/foia-annual-reports

U.S. Office of Personnel Management, "Job Analysis," webpage, undated. As of August 1, 2023:
https://www.opm.gov/policy-data-oversight/assessment-and-selection/job-analysis/

Vought, Russell T., acting director, Office of Management and Budget, Executive Office of the President, "Phase 1 Implementation of the Foundations for Evidence-Based Policymaking Act of 2018: Learning Agendas, Personnel, and Planning Guidance," memorandum for heads of executive departments and agencies, M-19-23, July 10, 2019.

Waterman, Robert H., Jr., Thomas J. Peters, and Julien R. Phillips, "Structure Is Not Organization," *Business Horizons*, Vol. 23, No. 3, June 1980.

W. K. Kellogg Foundation, *Logic Model Development Guide*, updated January 2004.

Yim, Randell A., managing director, homeland security and justice issues, U.S. Government Accountability Office, *Combating Terrorism: Evaluation of Selected Characteristics in National Strategies Related to Terrorism*, statement before the Subcommittee on National Security, Emerging Threats, and International Relations; Committee on Government Reform; U.S. House of Representatives, GAO-04-408T, February 3, 2004.

Zincir, Oya, and Ayşegül Özbebek Tunç, "An Imagination of Organizations in the Future: Rethinking McKinsey's 7S Model," in Roman Batko and Anna Szopa, eds., *Strategic Imperatives and Core Competencies in the Era of Robotics and Artificial Intelligence*, IGI Global Publishing, 2017.